MW01711430

THE SMILING PAWPAW

RONEL ENGELBRECHT
CHRIS RADEMEYER

ZEBRA

ZEBRA

Published by Zebra Press, an imprint of Southern Book Publishers
(a division of the New Holland Struik Publishing Group (Pty) Ltd)
PO Box 5563, Rivonia, 2128
E-mail: marikat@struik.co.za

First edition, first impression July 1999

Managing editor Marika Truter
Copy editors Hanneke Gagiano & Tracey Chalmers
Illustrator Prisma Graphics
Cover designer Lindy Truswell
Book designer Lindy Truswell & Patricia Crain
DTP Patricia Crain

Reproduction by PG&A, Cape Town
Printed and bound by CTP Book Printers (Pty) Ltd, PO Box 6060, Parow East, 7501

ISBN 1-86872-268-6

ACKNOWLEDGEMENTS

Writing this book started out as a serious project. As with everything else we do, the serious project turned into great fun.

We want to thank the following people for creating this experience:

- Marika Truter, our publisher: Your innovative and creative energy inspired us to take bold steps.
- Norman from The Boys, and Michael: You showed us a vision of what we can be.
- Marelize Steyn, make-up artist & stylist: You made us feel and look like royalty for one day.
- Everyone who discussed their experiences and ideas with us: We hope that others will benefit from your useful and practical approaches. (See Resource List on page 98.)

Ronel Engelbrecht & Chris Rademeyer

- Chris, my co-author and friend: Thank you for writing this book with me. Being with you gives me the freedom to be anything from a smiling pawpaw to whatever I can dream to be.
- Adele Mendelsohn: Thank you for assisting me with everything. Your ideas, enthusiasm, thoroughness and re-assurance are invaluable to me.

Ronel Engelbrecht

- Anne-Marie Raath: Thank you for your behind-the-scene efforts – you are really special.
- Louise Luttig: Thank you for your guidance, editing and professional input – and for struggling through my first draft.
- Tazana Morolo: Thank you for suffering through my handwriting and typing everything so professionally.
- Ronel, my partner in crime: Thank you for being you (so that I may be me) and for being there for me whenever I need you.
- I would like to acknowledge Him, who is always there for me.

Chris Rademeyer

CONTENTS

Introduction

1 Picking your fruit 1

2 Making the fruit salad 5

Getting started 8

Research your audience 9

The topic 16

Writing your presentation 25

Polishing and editing your presentation 33

Practising your delivery 39

3 Garnishing 45

Clothing 45

Body language 46

Posture, stance and movement 49

Communicating your understanding of the audience 49

Style 52

Your voice 53

Use space effectively 57

4 Psychobabble 59
The need for stress 59
Self-confidence 66
5 How to use the fruit shaker, and other tools 71
Static aids 74
Dynamic visual aids 74
Dos and don'ts 76
6 It's munchtime, folks 83
Establishing credibility and competence 86
Handling difficult situations 87
Questions 92
Pitfalls: how not to alienate your audience 95
It ain't over till it's over 96
Last words 96
7 Resource list 98

INTRODUCTION

The aim of *The Smiling Pawpaw* is to provide you with practical ideas and guidelines on presentations and to help you combine your own personal style with tried and tested know-how from the world of business presenting.

The book combines all the basic elements of good presenting, such as preparing a presentation and analysing the audience. It includes value-added topics, such as state-of-the-art presentation aids and how to find them. Here, at last, is just about everything a presenter needs to know.

In chapters 1 and 2 we focus on picking the fruit and making the fruit salad: where to start with preparing presentations and how to get going successfully. We focus on the importance of the audience and the necessity of researching and analysing the audience, how to handle them, how to start writing your presentation and formulating the central message.

Before you've spoken your first word, you've made your first impression by the way you're dressed and your body language. You can make your presentation that much stronger with the appropriate nonverbal communication. Chapter 3 explains how to use body language during your presentation, how to read your audience's body language, and how to control it or adapt to it.

Everybody suffers from nerves when presenting. We don't say that you should get rid of those butterflies, but rather that you let them fly in formation. Nervousness during presentations is as normal as breathing. In chapter 4 we will show you how to control it with confidence, instead of letting it control you.

Technology is the buzz-word for the new millennium. How can it help you? In chapter 5 we show you how to use available technology and how using the fruit shaker and other tools can make the difference between a good presentation and an excellent presentation.

It's munchtime, folks! In chapter 6 we whip the cream and add the cherry on top, showing you the vital differences between the Smiling Pawpaw and the Fresh Funky Fruit.

Throughout the book, the conniving Smiling Pawpaw and the honest Fresh Funky Fruit will respectively give you less appropriate methods – and sometimes downright suicidal ones – and more appropriate presentation behaviour. Follow the Fresh Funky Fruit for lifesaving guidance on your presentation journey – do not dare to follow the Smiling Pawpaw's rotten advice.

Giving presentations is not only about developing skills; it's also about performing. We cannot all be perfect presenters, but we can all put on an outstanding show. We can do it the funkiest and most exciting way possible.

So, go out and make the freshest, funkiest and most fruitful presentation ever!

Enjoy!

The authors

PICKING YOUR FRUIT 1

In the 1996 Olympic Games the whole world's attention was focussed on one man and one race: the 100 m final. Linford Christie was the favourite to become the fastest man on earth. He promised not only himself but also the world that his final race would be gold and not silver as in the previous Olympic Games. His performance in the heats pointed not only to a win but most probably a record.

The time came for the race.

Three times Linford Christie jumped the gun, which resulted in his disqualification. He had to watch from the side of the track as someone else won what should have been his.

We often perform just like Christie: well prepared for our big moment, at peak performance level, but then we keep on jumping the gun and end up disqualified.

Whether in the corporate world or an organisation, each one of us gets an opportunity to take part in the race, often in the arena of presentations. The moment you are up there and have to speak your piece, you see that crowd of faces staring back, you trip, or jump the gun, or freeze, or carry on and slowly die out there – with everyone watching.

And boy, does it get hot out there!

It can be excruciatingly uncomfortable to do a presentation. You may feel that if you were to open your mouth whatever you would say would come out sounding stupid. (It's Murphy's Law of course: when something can go wrong, it will!)

Ask us: we've been there. Even today, we still learn and make mistakes. Take me (Chris) for example. Whilst busy writing this book, I had to do a presentation. Nothing out of the ordinary, just a very important public relations project. After a dramatic entrance and an even more dramatic start, I knew I had captured my audience's attention. It was now time to build up to a highly charged appeal to the audience. Have you ever seen a cheese soufflé falling flat? I have. A cellphone rang very close to me. I was instantly annoyed, mumbling, 'What absolute rudeness!' And then it hit me: it was my own phone ringing, in my pocket!

What a way of disqualifying myself by undermining my professional stature, my composure and my credibility.

There are more ways than one to get yourself disqualified, such as by:

- not taking on any presentations, convinced that you cannot and will not ever be able to deliver a presentation;
- comparing yourself to others, especially well-known professional presenters and entertainers such as Larry King, Mike Lipkin or Evita Bezuidenhout;
- rigidly following the 'rules' of presenting without developing an individual approach;
- not utilising the skills that may make you a good presenter; and
- not practising enough.

Experts on presenting say that it can be more frightening to some people than death. People who have a fear of presenting experience a variety of symptoms: cold sweat, dry mouth, sweaty palms, uneven heartbeat, difficulty in breathing, and even nausea and memory loss.

Some of the world's most renowned presenters admit to being nervous. Most good presenters were once bad presenters. After all, you have to start somewhere, don't you?

Mark Twain sums it up the best: 'There are two types of presenters: those who are nervous and those who lie.'

Everybody, it doesn't matter how experienced, faces some form of anxiety. The best way to deal with this anxiety is to acknowledge it and to realise that you are not unique in feeling so. And there is a sure way to reduce this fear: prepare and practise, over and over. It is much like riding a bicycle: you have to fall off a few times, get up again, try again, fall off, practise some more, get the wobbles sorted out, and then one day you can say, 'Wow, I can ride!'

If the fear of presenting causes you to prepare more, this fear serves as its own antidote.

Remember, those who fail to prepare are preparing for failure – so prepare, prepare, prepare.

Business today is leaning more on the individual's skills, and presentation skills often develop as part of one's job. It does not matter whether you are a manager or in the sales, advertising, marketing, information or planning division. You will, every once in a while, have to make a presentation, even if it is just to introduce someone, or to make a farewell speech to a member at the golf club's year-end function.

Of course, it cannot hurt to possess some natural skill for the job. Some people have a flair for presenting and talking in general. It certainly comes easier to some than to others. But if you are one of the disadvantaged majority, remember that presenting is a skill that you can refine and develop.

Being naturally skilled at business presentations is not always good enough. One needs to develop and nurture such skills.

MAKING THE FRUIT SALAD 2

Let's now consider what is necessary to refine and develop the perfect mix for the perfect presentation.

It is vital not only to analyse but also to understand your audience, even before you write one word of your presentation. The audience should be the key focus of your presentation – their understanding of what you are trying to put across will make or break the presentation.

Your goal as presenter is to be perceived by the audience as credible and qualified to discuss the topic.

Try to impress your audience and make a fool of yourself. To put it simply, if your audience gets the idea that you don't know what you're talking about, they will stop listening.

You must always be able to read and adapt to any audience you come across.

Because audiences differ, a well-prepared presentation given to the wrong audience will be as ineffective as a poorly prepared presentation given to the right audience.

Audiences are not objective: they have preconceived ideas about you and the topic. That may be because of cultural, perceptual or semantic differences, or differences in style between you and them, or it may be because of the reason why they are attending the presentation.

There can be any number of reasons why members of your audience are attending: they want to be there, they are forced to be there, they have paid, or they might know you.

Think of the last presentation you attended as a member of the audience. What was your reason for going? How would you have changed that presentation to match your expectations?

Many speakers will tell you that South African audiences are some of the most unpredictable they have ever come across in the world. This makes South African audiences sometimes difficult to understand and to deal with.

In general, South African audiences don't like to participate in the same manner as some overseas audiences during a presentation. One very seldom sees a South African audience doing a singalong and jumping up and down when requested. They are a bit more reserved than their counterparts in other countries. South African audiences might be different to those in other countries because of the diversity of their cultural backgrounds.

You might also find South African audiences inconsiderate at times. For instance, some people still seem to think it is quite acceptable to answer their cellphone or accept messages by various interesting means during a presentation.

The story goes that a young, newly appointed executive decided to visit all the small towns where his company had branches. During a presentation at one branch office, the receptionist twice used the intercom system to announce the arrival of fresh home-baked vetkoek, after which half of the group disappeared.

The lesson learnt from this is to expect anything and to be prepared to deal with it. That will help you to plan ahead so you are flexible enough to deal with any eventuality; if you cannot do so, you will lose focus and fluff badly.

Much of a presenter's anxiety stems from not knowing enough about the topic or audience. Because of this you may try to survive out there by projecting an image, rather than conveying your message effectively. As a result, you could be peeled and eaten like a litchi!

We all know the toffee-apple presenters. They look competent and bright on the outside, but boy do we know what to expect from the inside if they start to talk!

Let's all admit that we are worried about our image. We, for instance, went on a diet to be 'shipshape' for the photograph on the back of this book!

To overcome the image problem, you have to build your self-confidence. There is only one way of doing that: you must believe that you know your audience and your topic. Make sure that you are credible as a speaker.

Credibility in the eyes of your audience is achieved by delivering your topic in a meaningful way. This self-confidence does not make the presentation, however. You have to project the right image, the image of an expert who knows the topic and makes it understandable and interesting.

You must research and plan before you can have a well-written and well-structured presentation that will capture and hold the attention of your audience.

GETTING STARTED

Presentation planning is most effective if you start organising your efforts right from the beginning.

Open a file

Get yourself a preparation sheet to work on. This sheet will be your planning and development sheet. Once you've planned a section, you will write down the key aspects. Part of presentation success lies in organising the presentation. This is the recipe for the fruity presentation.

This file should also contain the organisational details of the presentation. For instance, when and where is the presentation? If it is in the morning, at a breakfast, this will determine the atmosphere. Look at your presentation from your audience's perspective. What will be on their minds? Perhaps your audience had to get up two hours earlier and face the M1. So, be short and specific. With the aroma of eggs and bacon wafting about, you don't want to spoil the eating part.

At a very formal conference, your presentation might be slotted in just before the tea break. Think back. How do you usually feel before a tea break when somebody starts their presentation?

When you start, behave like an investigative journalist and consider who, where, when, what and how.

- **Who?**
  Find out about your audience.

- **Where?**
  Exact physical address of the venue and contact numbers of the organisers. Which parking lot should you use for easy access? In which room/hall/conference venue will your presentation take place?

- **When?**
  The time and date.

- **What?**
  The topic and any specific angle or ideas that the organiser may have.

- **How?**
  What is available?
  Will you do it on a stage or sitting down?
  What type of microphone is available? If it's a clip-on microphone and you're a woman then have a belt available, otherwise you will have to stand with the 'box' in your hand.
  What technology is available?
  How will the audience be seated? In rows or around tables?
  How long should you speak?
  Will there be other speakers?
  Where do you fit in the programme?

RESEARCH YOUR AUDIENCE

Well, you could always ignore your audience! The only problem is they might not ignore you. Remember one golden rule: never give a presentation with a chip on your shoulder. If you had one bad presentation experience before, don't let that show to the entire audience. You cannot present successfully feeling sorry for yourself. The audience will sense that straight away and will have you for breakfast, lunch and dinner. You have to go out there and project self-confidence and charisma.

The first place to research your audience is to put yourself in their shoes: put your audience's feelings and needs first. Audiences are self-centred. They care more about their own feelings, emotions and needs than those of anybody else. It is important to them that they feel their basic needs are being addressed. Your audience can understand your subject only by relating it to their own ideas, problems and experiences. Approach the subject from their perspective, not yours. Explain how they can benefit or how they will be affected by what you are saying. Show them what they will gain.

The closer you get to that, the easier it will be to keep their attention, deliver your message and walk out of there – alive. Even if they disagree with you, you would have built credibility and trust.

Ignore your audience and focus only on what you will gain. The fact that they're supposed to listen to you means nothing!

Because of cultural differences and diversity, we don't always attach the same meaning to a communicated message. Perfect sharing of meaning is hardly possible. Consider the word 'chair'. What you think of and what the next person sees may be light-years apart. You may picture a basic kitchen model while the next person imagines a luxurious wingback chair.

Communication barriers play a role in any presentation: it's almost like picking fruit through a chicken-wire fence. As presenter, you must be aware of them and must make an effort to deal with them. This will only be possible if you know who you are talking to. This could easily be influenced by the size of your audience. The size of the audience won't affect your topic, but it will affect the delivery method and your approach. The number of people in the audience will determine how easy or difficult it is to get to know them.

The way you handle your audience will give you a leading edge and also credibility. The size of the audience determines your approach.

The large audience

The larger your audience, the more 'general' things become. For a large audience, you can make more general assumptions. A big group shares a great diversity of views which you will have to accommodate. A large crowd tends to think that you have to entertain them. You have to make them feel good about themselves. You have to cater for their needs. To do that, you must surprise them. Excite them. Wake them up.

> *The larger the audience, the more dramatic you have to make your presentation, almost as if you were giving a show.*

You could start with a dramatic announcement, or act out something. By doing this, you will not only surprise them, but most probably impress them. They will be more likely to remember your message. To influence their way of thinking, it is important to appeal to the emotions of a large audience.

A presenter once had the disadvantage of the last time-slot in a two-day workshop. The audience was tired. He knew that. His topic was 'How to realise the best in yourself!' He started by switching off all the lights. A moment later, crackers and small indoor fireworks went off. During all this excitement, he played his theme song, 'You're simply the best.' Needless to say, his audience was wide awake and ready to hear what he had to say. You don't have to go to such lengths, but be bold!

You can't be sure of the larger audience's knowledge of your topic. It will be very difficult to know how much they already know or how they feel about the topic. It is impossible to determine their attitude and beliefs regarding the subject. You have to assume what they know, how much they know, and how they feel about it. It will be almost impossible for you to have some insight into the audience's broad characteristics, such as their age, gender, religious beliefs, educational background, financial status or even their reason for being there.

This information, however, could help you with the angle of your presentation. So you will have to generalise and make assumptions about their characteristics. Your message will be to the general public, the masses. Think of presenting to an audience that fills a rugby stadium, an Ellis Park of people. You'll talk differently to them than to ten people at work.

Even if a few hundred people in your audience don't quite agree with your opinion, they might still appreciate your openness, your way of reasoning and your viewpoint. The others might even love you.

Be careful not to offend anyone: the bigger the group, the greater the danger of doing so. It's much easier to tell a sensitive joke to ten people at work than to tell the same joke to your rugby stadium audience. The possibility of offending one person is 60 000 times greater.

Stay with your original presentation and idea. Don't try to change it during your presentation just because you feel the audience will respond better.

The small audience

The smaller the audience, the more specific you have to be. With a small audience you have to work much harder to reach every individual. The biggest advantage of the small group is that you can emphasise reason and offer solid information by detailed one-to-one discussions, which would be impossible with a larger group.

People in a small group tend to have a certain group cohesiveness. They cannot disappear in a crowd of people. They will tend to pay closer attention to what you have to say and, because they feel more exposed, they will not risk daydreaming.

The smaller the group, the more control you have. However, it becomes easier for them to challenge you. You should expect that possibility and be able to deal with it.

Depending on your topic, aspects like age, gender, education, culture or religion might have an influence on your approach and delivery. These characteristics will also determine your examples and the details that you focus on.

Take age for example. With a younger audience, you have to be more careful of the type of examples you use. Younger audiences have more limited life experience: they may not fully understand your examples. Gender is another aspect to consider. Do you still remember the embarrassing moment when F W de Klerk called Frene Ginwala, the Speaker of Parliament, 'Sir'?

If you present a very academic topic, know the audience's academic background. You might lose them by talking over their heads, or by making them feel like Grade 1 children.

Learn more about your audience

How can you learn more about your audience?

- Use your common sense.
- Talk to the organiser and person who invited you.
- If there is a public relations section which can shed light on the audience, contact it.

- If you know people who will be in the audience, talk to them.
- Talk to secretaries, they are a wonderful source of information.
- Read about the company or department.
- If possible, visit the company or department before you prepare your presentation.
- Talk to previous presenters.
- Be creative and use some imagination.

The larger audience requires a different approach to the smaller audience. Whereas you can be very specific about things with a smaller audience, this may be dangerous with a large audience. The only South African presenter who we know of to get away with everything is Evita Bezuidenhout. Only she can attack and openly call a spade a spade and get paid for it!

Never give the same presentation twice. Use the same information, but remember no two audiences are alike. Some members might be in both groups and you will become so blasé with the subject that you lose credibility.

Now that you know more about your audience, write down the key elements that will have an influence on your delivery to the ten people at work and the rugby stadium audience.

EXAMPLE OF AN AUDIENCE CHECKLIST WORKSHEET

Specific needs or feelings the audience might have

1 ....
2 ....
3 ....
4 ....

Characteristics

Prior knowledge
Unusual characteristics
Size
Language
Gender
Age
Religious beliefs
Educational background
Financial status
Position in organisation

Information about the organisation

1 ....
2 ....
3 ....
4 ....

Information about the department/division

1 ....
2 ....
3 ....
4 ....

Other relevant comments

....
....

Now that you know and understand your audience, it is important to give them something to listen to.

THE TOPIC

If your presentation will be in a social setting where you have some say on the topic, decide on a topic that you know and that will mean something to your audience and will not evoke a response of, 'Oh no, not another presentation on the topic of presentations!' Remember your own background influences your ideas about the topic. Always reflect back on your audience and their perspective. Always keep your topic practical and contemporary. If you have no idea where to start, you could browse for General Topics on the Internet. These are some useful websites:

HELPFUL WEBSITES

Argus Clearing house
http://www.clearinghouse.net
This clearing house is organised by topical guides.

Lycos' Sites by Subject
http://www.lycos.com/
An alphatabetical list provides options to a variety of general interesting topics.

Yahoo!
http://www.yahoo.com
This is one of the best websites for browsing topical lists of various subjects. It focusses on numerous topics, including computers and Internet, education, entertainment, government, health, recreation, reference, regional, science, social science, society and culture.

If your presentation will be in a business environment, the organisers (or your boss) will most probably set the topic. Companies don't have the money or time simply to arrange presentations and have someone talking about whatever catches their fancy.

The organiser of the event may have set an *open* topic where you are given only a vague idea of the content, such as 'Presentations in industry'.

With *directed* topics you are given some direction and more detail about the expected content, such as 'Presentations in the advertising industry'.

Specific topics clearly state the expected content, such as 'Presentations in the advertising industry with specific regard to pitching for new clients'; and they require a much more focussed approach from your side.

The recipe your presentation will follow depends on how detailed the topic was formulated. With a general topic you have to stick to the recipe: the core message that you want to convey.

It is more difficult to prepare a specific topic but easier to convey the message. However, the more specific the topic, the easier it will be for you to disappoint your audience, or the easier it will be for them to drive you into a corner if you don't perform.

Once you have clarity about your topic, you will have to research your topic.

Researching your topic

Free your mind. Some of your most creative and inspiring ideas might come in the bath, or while driving. Think wide – think very wide. This is the only time that you can forget about your audience. Jot down as many ideas as possible. Sleep on your topic if you can. The making of an exquisite fruit salad requires standing time.

Mind-mapping

Mind-mapping will also be useful when practising your presentation. It will help you to remember and understand your topic much easier.

Use mind-mapping to free up your thought processes and to develop ideas.

This time around it will need to be more specific, but will stimulate your brain to think creatively. It's also good for question-and-answer sessions during your presentation. By using this technique, you will ensure that your message will always be focussed.

So, how does mind-mapping work?

- Take a sheet of plain white paper.
- Draw a small block or picture of your topic in the centre of the page.
- To generate ideas about your topic, write down key words, linked by spokes radiating from the central picture. Write only single words – the first ones that come to mind – and keep all spokes connected to the central picture.
- Free-associate rapidly by writing down any idea that comes into your head and don't edit any ideas. Write down as many ideas as possible. See these ideas as branches growing from a tree, spreading out on the paper.
- Once you run out of ideas concerning your main picture, repeat the process with your key words. Radiate subthoughts from each of the key words.
- Once this is complete, look for patterns and associations between ideas. Link all connected ideas with the same colour, but use a different colour for each group of ideas. (See mind-map 1.)
- Redraw your map, leaving out any irrelevant ideas and grouping all related ideas together. You should now have several important concepts relating to your topic. You can add further information to the edge of your mind-map. (See mind-map 2.)

You may even have developed a structure for presenting these ideas.

MIND-MAP 1: plotting down all possible ideas

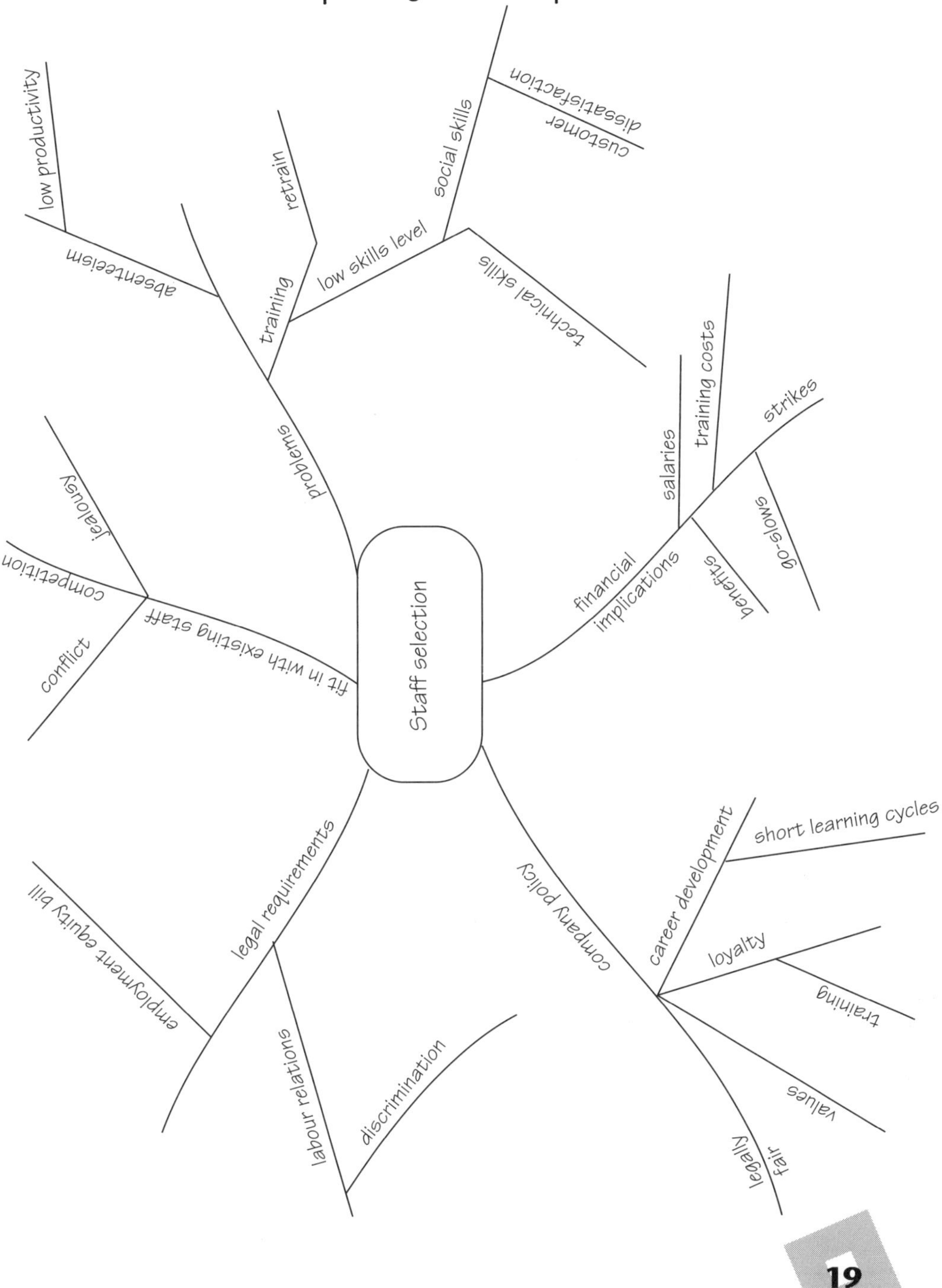

MIND-MAP 2: organising your ideas

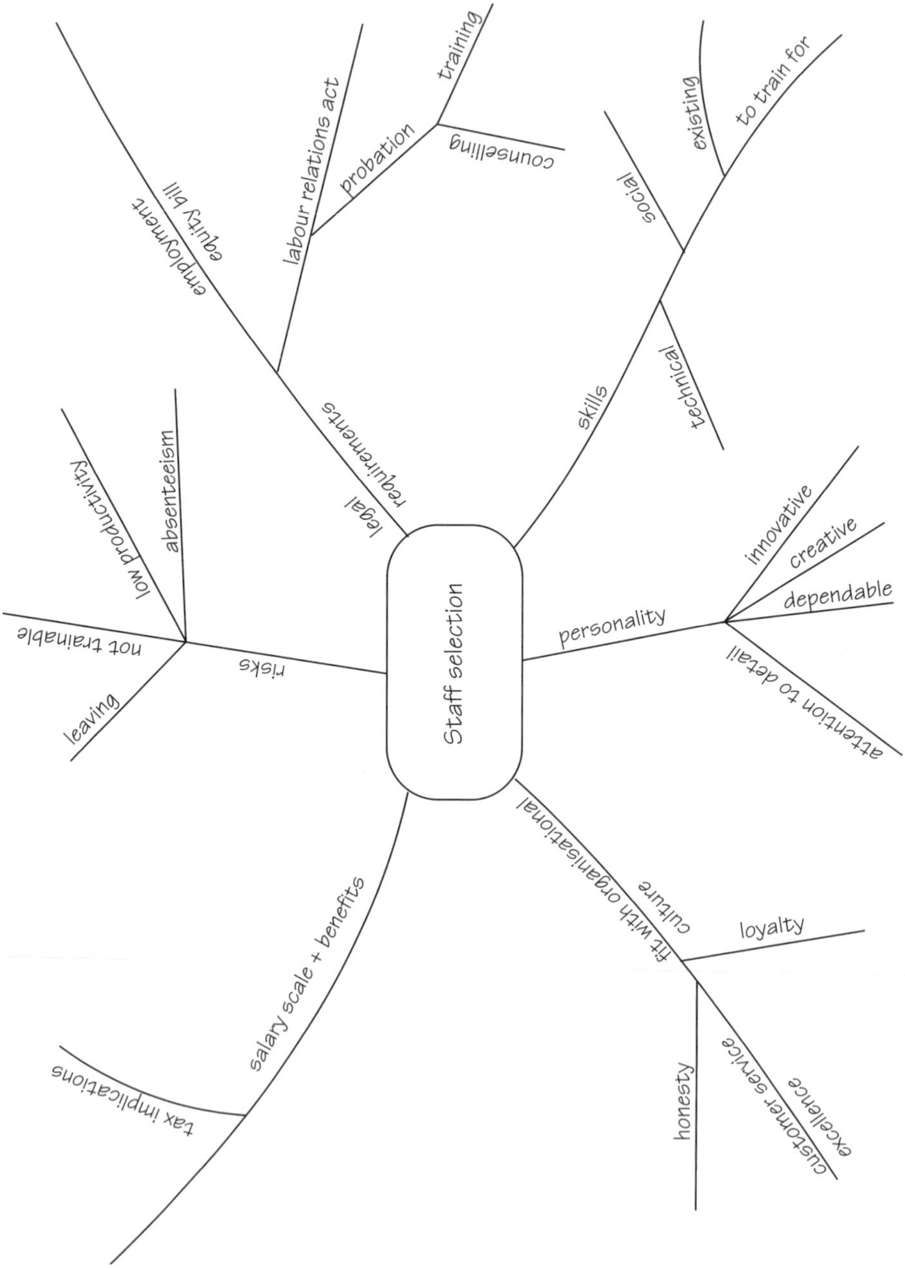

Remember that this is a process which requires a lot of time and thought. Do not rush it.

To practise mind-mapping, take a topic like 'A fruity presentation' and see what you come up with.

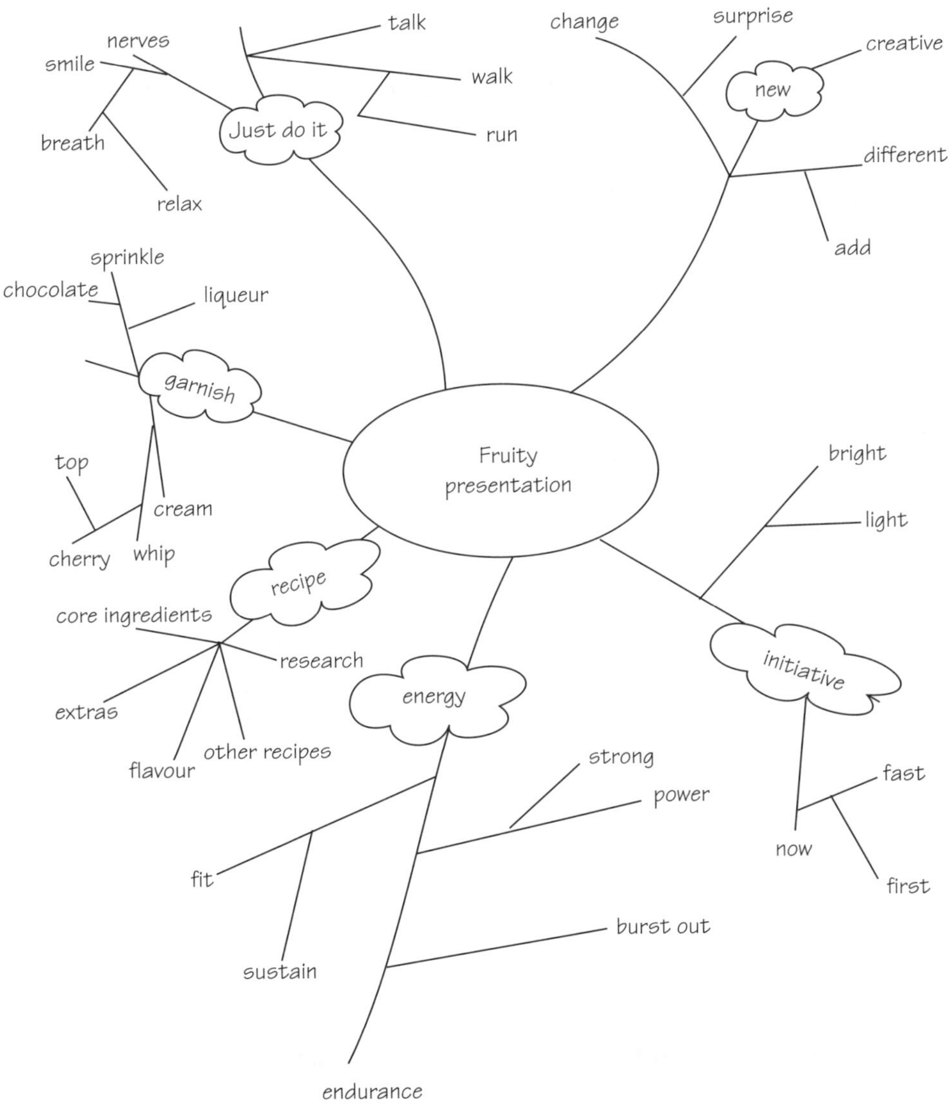

Other resources

After generating initial ideas, take your research one step further with the use of other resources. It's not only your own thoughts and ideas that will help you. Use magazines, newspapers and the Internet for interesting ideas, one-liners, opening statements, analogies, etc. The world is full of ideas and information. Don't disregard any. A very important point to remember is not to edit anything while gathering your information. This will mean overediting right from the beginning. You have to get as much information as possible, so that you don't have gaps to fill later on. These are some useful Internet search tools:

HELFPUL WEBSITES

Alta Vista
http://www.altavista.digital.com
Alta Vista searches for Web pages or Usenet groups, which makes it one of the most powerful keyword search engines.

Excite
wttp://www.excite.com
Excite will perform concept or keyword searches in a natural language approach. It will also locate Usenet groups. You can further tailor your search to find sites that have been reviewed by topical areas. The topics are arranged hierarchically.

Galaxy
http://www.einet.net/cgi-bin/wais-text-multi?
Galaxy is one of the most comprehensive search engines because you can tell it to search Gopher and Telnet sites, as well as pages on the Web. If you are not used to using

Boolean search tools, you can simply click buttons to refine your search.

Lycos
http:/www.lycos.com/
Lycos is Greek for 'spider'. 'Spider' is an Internet term for an automated program that scans the Web to locate index sites. Try the customised search option to use Boolean search tools easily. You can limit your search by using its hierarchy of topics. Lycos will also enable you to search for sound and picture files.

If none of these search engines lead you to the information you're looking for, newspapers or netzines may lead you to alternative sites.

Total News
http://www.totalnews.com/
A one-stop site for finding various media outlets, including FOX News, MSNBC, CNN Interactive, CBS News, USA Today, ABC Radio, National Public Radio, Reuters, and TIME Daily and South African news desks.

Associated Press
http://www.csmonitor.com/headlines/apfeed/apfeed.html
The headlines from Associated Press.

The Economist
http://www/economist.com/index.html
British magazine for discussion of a broad range of international topics.

Forbes Magazine
http://www.forbes.com/
Economic news from a business perspective – it calls itself a 'capitalist tool'.

Foreign Affairs
http://foreignaffairs.org/
Prestigious journal that focusses on international policy.

Time Warner's Pathfinder Network
http://www.pathfinder.com/
Current issues of *Time* and various other periodicals such as *Money, Life* and netzines.

USNews and World Report
http://www.usnews.com/
Weekly news journal.

Free Internet Encyclopaedia
http://clever.net/cam/encyclopedia.html
Organised by micro and macro reference areas and arranged alphabetically.

Books Online
http://www.cs.cmu.edu/Web/bookauthors.html
Scroll down the alphabetical list of authors. Good for finding classics that have been digitised.

Libweb
http://sunsite.berkeley.edu/Libweb?
Provides links to hundreds of library collections around the world.

WRITING YOUR PRESENTATION

After generating information through mind-mapping, research and other resources, you can structure and write your presentation. In doing this you have to:

- Formulate the goal of the presentation.
- Formulate your central message.
- Structure your presentation.
- Write the body.
- Write the conclusion.
- Write the introduction.
- Connect the parts.

Goal of your presentation

What do you want to achieve with your presentation?

The body of knowledge on presenting refers to the goal of a presentation. This goal could be to inform, to persuade or to entertain. We like to refer to these aspects as the elements of your presentation goal. Any presentation should inform. If it does not provide new information, it should at least reinforce previously known information.

Any presentation will persuade or influence the audience in one way or another. Even if members of the audience disagree with the content, it means that their own beliefs and values were reinforced. For a presentation to be effective in the Information Age, it needs some element of entertainment.

Exercise:
Write down the goal you want to achieve with both a large audience and a small audience about ways to improve the standard of service in South Africa. What you want to tell your two audiences might differ.

1 ....

2 ....

Your goal might be to persuade your audience to improve their business practices in a way which will help raise South African standards of service.

Formulating your central message

You now have a goal, but will your audience listen to you? You have to find a way for the audience to remember that one main thought you want to share with them. You cannot stuff their heads full of a large number of startling ideas, unless you are spending several hours with them. They only have the capacity to hang on to one big thought. The biggest sin of presenting is trying to sell an audience everything at once.

You want the audience to remember the most important idea: your central message.

How can they do that if you kill them with information? Be as selective about your central message as possible. Do this even before you start to write your presentation.

To formulate your central message, break down your topic into two or three parts.

On your preparation sheet, write down the exact wording of your central message. The key to getting it right is to ensure that it is exact. Don't have any airy, fuzzy wording. If some of the parts in this message are still unclear, go back and get more information. Your central message might look something like this:

'By the end of our book, we want our readers to understand that the three most important aspects of a good presentation are research, planning and delivery.'

'By the end of this presentation, management must vote for increasing the profit margins in the organisation through unbundling, retrenchment and outsourcing.'

Now that you have your central message, you should start structuring your information.

Structuring your presentation

Once you have determined the goal of your presentation and you have settled on your central message, you have to organise your information into some structure. This structure should also reinforce the approach you want to take with your presentation. As you structure your information, you will have to select certain chunks and discard others. You have to do this structuring process with your audience profile and your goal and central message in mind.

How you organise and structure your presentation depends on your personality and what will work for you. But always keep your audience in mind.

The first golden rule: people are naturally inclined to understand things in terms of their parts. Most things are broken down into three parts: past, present, future; breakfast, lunch, supper; morning, afternoon, evening; beginning, middle, end.

People need some sort of organising structure to give meaning to information. If you don't organise your central message into some sort of cohesive structure, then the audience will attempt to do it for you. The time they use to do this is the time that they don't listen to your message.

At the start of your presentation, give your audience a structure with information they will need to understand the central message. This will help your audience recognise a logical flow. A well-structured presentation will definitely have a greater impact on the audience than a poorly structured one.

The body

Structure the body of your presentation first. This contains the bulk of your information and should be the most detailed.

The most important aspect to remember is to tell your audience what you want to tell them!

The second golden rule is KISS: Keep It Short and Simple. Don't use fillers, you will lose the audience.

There are some basic strategies to use when you structure the body of your presentation. These strategies include the:

- **topical:** according to main headings
- **chronological:** develop an easy-to-follow structure
- **motivational:** psychological steps of gaining attention, establishing a need, satisfying it, and visualising the results

- **residual:** eliminate all alternatives and argue for the remaining option
- **cause and effect:** show the results
- **visual:** map ideas visually
- **classical judicial:** use argument and counter-argument
- **problem solving:** analyse what is wrong with the situation and what should be done to correct it
- **compare and contrast:** compare advantages and disadvantages of one situation with another.

Once you have a better understanding of what you are going to say in the body of your presentation, you should concern yourself with the beginning and end of your presentation. The beginning and end will most likely be the aspects the audience will remember best. Because of their important role in a presentation, you cannot start developing them before establishing the body of your presentation.

You must have a complete idea of what you will be saying before working on the conclusion and introduction.

The conclusion

Use the conclusion to wrap up your thoughts, ideas and arguments. Reach your conclusion in a dramatic fashion to give your audience a sense of having made a discovery.

The golden rule is never to add any new ideas to your conclusion. Simply try to summarise your presentation.

The following are important in the conclusion:

- Inform the audience that you are about to close
- Reinforce the central message
- Provide a sense of closure of some sort
- Summarise the main ideas
- Don't give new information: review the old points
- Refer to your introduction
- Leave the audience with something to remember.

Methods of concluding include:

- **Summary of the presentation:** paraphrase the central message of the presentation
- **Personal intention:** give a personal undertaking as to what you will do next
- **Call for action:** ask the audience for commitment
- **Compare and contrast:** point out the advantages and disadvantages of following the proposed solution.

If possible, leave your conclusion until after the question-and-answer session. This will give you the advantage of having the last say. A novice presenter may, however, feel more at ease concluding and then facing the question-and-answer session. As a novice, you want to survive the first few presentations and do not need the extra demands of changing your well-prepared conclusion on the spot as a result of profound questions that were raised by a well-informed audience.

End with a bang, not a whimper. This is the lasting impression that you leave with the audience. If this is done poorly, your audience will be left with a very low opinion of your credibility.

The introduction

Write this part of the presentation last. Be creative. Gain the audience's attention. Start with a grabber. Use an anecdote, outrageous statistics, a relevant story, a quotation, a personal observation or humour. Then focus the attention on your central message by making a clear statement about your topic and by giving a quick preview of your main ideas. Establish your credibility and build rapport.

Use the introduction to grab the audience's attention and make them want to listen to your presentation. The introduction is your public relations exercise about your presentation. By the end of the introduction the audience should know, without a doubt, what you are going to talk about.

Tips for developing an effective introduction:

- Keep it brief
- Reveal the topic
- Use effective attention-grabbers
- Preview your main arguments and ideas
- Establish credibility
- Tell the audience why they should listen to you.

You could tell a story or anecdote to begin your presentation. Make sure that it is relevant to your topic.

> *If you really want to confuse your audience from the start, tell a story with no connection to the topic whatsoever.*

You may want to start with humour, but only if it's appropriate and natural. You could also use a good quote. Consider the possibility of a shock statement: 'Eighty per cent of you sitting here today will have AIDS. That is, if we don't do something about educating people about the disease.' This was a statement made by a nurse at a school. You can be sure that the audience listened to her! You could compliment your business audience by telling them you know what the group's profit was.

Humour directed at yourself might not always work. Telling a joke just to break the ice could leave you looking like a bad stand-up comedian. However, doing or saying something totally unexpected could be quite effective. 'Let's all go home, I've got nothing to say . . . well that's what you think about this topic. Surprise, ...'

A series of questions at the start of the presentation will engage the audience. You can also design your questions to preview the main points that you are going to develop. You can either use direct questions to elicit a response from the audience, or you can use rhetorical questions.

Whatever you do, make sure it will engage your audience and that you feel comfortable to do it. Mr Mandela uses humour very effectively in his presentations. In his final speech at the opening of Parliament in 1999 he said the following: 'I urge you to remember the impressive performance I've made so far. Many of my age start coughing after the first sentence . . . in a few months I will be standing next to the road saying: "Please help, unemployed, no money, new wife".'

Connections

To smooth out your presentation, you need connections or transitions that link one idea to another. This is a verbal way of making your presentation flow. It is important that your introduction, middle and conclusion form a complete whole. The various parts of the presentation must be connected.

Use words or phrases to tie all the ideas together, such as:

- Firstly, secondly, finally
- To continue with this argument
- This issue (just mentioned)

- The matter referred to previously
- Next, I want to.

When you want to introduce something new to your audience, you could, for example, say: 'I'd like to start this part off by ...' or 'I think that you will agree that ...'.

Connectives are bridges between your different sections. You need to lead your audience from idea to idea verbally. You should help them understand how your ideas fit together and form a unit.

Sometimes single words or short phrases can be used, such as 'and', 'therefore', 'likewise', 'more importantly', 'in contrast with', or 'in comparison to'.

Always keep your audience in mind. Don't confuse them with abbreviations or unfamiliar language. Companies and departments frequently develop their own internal language that is totally incomprehensible to the rest of Planet Earth. What would you think if an executive asked a group of female employees whether their PMS in the first cycle is up to date? Would it be clear to you that he is simply enquiring after the Performance Management Schedules of the first quarter? Know your audience and adapt your language accordingly.

Once you have established your central message and have the body, conclusion and introduction in place, the time has come to edit your work. This is your chance to make it even sharper and to simplify your phrases even more. It's time to eliminate fluff and give your presentation the *woema* it needs!

POLISHING AND EDITING YOUR PRESENTATION

When you start to write, remember that your first draft will not be the last. In fact, it should not be! For a good result, redo and edit the content at least three times. Be your own worst critic.

Polishing your presentation means writing, rewriting, editing, taking out and adding (although not necessarily in that order). By polishing your presentation, you'll also get to know your content better.

Keep in mind that editing does not mean only cutting out: it also involves rethinking, rewriting and restructuring.

Be consistent and concise. Cut out all redundant points and add on where needed. Focus on your audience and measure your content, your goal and their needs against one another. This will guide you in your editing.

Now is the time to go through all the information with a sharp eye. Pick out all the good fruit and discard the rest. F W de Klerk's speech calling on South Africans to register for the 1999 elections is a good example of excellent word choice and idea development. He not only uses strong words, but also uses them very effectively: 'I want to motivate you all to fight this sense of withdrawal, and urge people to become more involved . . . unless you do so, this whole process can be derailed and can become unstuck. This new South Africa, warts and all, is a much better place.'

Plan ahead for questions. Anticipate some likely questions and prepare answers. This will make you feel more comfortable and in control.

To write a memorable and dynamic presentation you have to do it with style. Let your audience see what you say. Sketch them pictures in their minds. Make them as colourful as possible. Give your audience enough examples to help them generate some visual concepts for themselves.

You can use statistics for impact. Make all the statistics as real as possible for the audience. For example, 'while you are reading this book, there are thousands of people out there now who suffer doing a presentation'. But it is also important to put statistics in simple terms: not 999 999 people, but thousands, or use analogies such as 'enough people to fill Ellis Park'.

The words that you select have a dramatic impact on your audience's reaction to both your ideas and effectiveness as presenter. Use power and command words to get their attention and to give the impression of confidence and competence. This will include phrases such as: 'I'm certain about...', 'It is definite that ...', 'My research shows that ...'.

To ensure your audience retains the essence of your message, repeat your main ideas in various formats.

When writing down your presentation do not produce a word-for-word account unless it is going to be used in handouts. A verbatim text could lead you into the trap of reading a presentation, instead of presenting it. You do not want to join the ranks of those sing-along-with-Fred presenters. A presentation written in short phrases will help you to assume a conversational tone or get you talking instead of speechifying.

When you deliver your presentation, a comfortable style will provide you with a more relaxed environment to manifest your own personality.

These are some useful websites for adding the final touches:

HELPFUL WEBSITES

Bartlett's Familiar Quotations
http://www.cc.columbia.eu/acis/bartleby/bartlett/
Need a quote for your presentation? Get it online from this classic source.

Online English Grammar
http://www.edunet.com/english/grammar/index.html
This page is associated with the Digital Education Network. The English Grammar Clinic provides answers to common problems on grammatical form.

The Purdue University Writing Lab
http://owl.english.purdue.edu
Useful source for writing tools.

Strunk & White: *The elements of style*
http://www.columbia.edu/acis/bartleby/strunk
Do you have a grammatical question or concern about written format? You may find the answer here.

What is?
http://whatiscom/
Use this handy reference to speak the language of computer geeks. You can scroll through a top frame of alphabetic terms or search using Excite.

A semantic rhyming dictionary
http://www.cs.cmu.edu/~dougb/rhyme.html
Type in a search word and you can see if there is a perfect match, a syllable rhyme or a homophone.

WWWebster Dictionary
http://www.m-w.com/netdict.htm
This the online version of the Merriam-Webster dictionary. You can search for phrases as well as words.

The World Wide Web acronym and abbreviation server
http://www.ucc.ie/info/net/acronymys/
In addition to finding the meaning of an acronym, this database allows you to type in words to determine if they are included in an acronym.

Brewer's dictionary of phrase and fable
http:/www.mk.net/~dt/Bibliomania/Reference/PhraseAndFable
Popular in hardcover since 1879, there now is a hypertext version. Use the alphabetic method of browsing or go to the main Bibliomania page to search at http://www.bibliomania.com

Logos
http://www.logos.it/query.html/
Non sole parole? You can search for words and phrases from around the world at this source.

A Shakespearean glossary
http://english-www.hss.cmu.edu/langs/shakespear-glossary.
Stuck on a phrase attributed to the Bard? You may find it here in this alphabetic listing of words from Shakespeare, forsooth!

Wordbot
http://www.cs.washington.edu/homes/kgolden/wordbot.html
This is a robot that will find translations of words from a wide range of languages.

The Daily Muse
http://www.cais.net/aschnedr/muse
Humorous commentary and jokes about current news stories can be found here.

Clean up your presentation

It's important not to overkill your presentation. We sometimes think that the more elaborate the choice of words, the higher the impact. If the following expressions are used sparsely, they can be useful and effective; however repetition and over-use will strip your presentation of impact.

Exaggerate:
'It is absolutely and positively essential . . .'
'It is true beyond any possible shadow of doubt . . .'

Use trite expressions:
'As you can see . . .'
'At grassroots level . . .'
'Move the goalposts . . .'
'They say . . .'
'Level the playing field . . .'
When using these stale phrases, you will immediately get a bad response.

Use grouping expressions:
'What I'm trying to get at . . .'
'What I want to say . . .'

If you need some help with issues of grammar style, or if you are looking for an appropriate quotation, there are numerous websites that might give you some ideas. Some of them are listed on pages 36–38. To prepare visual aids that will complement your presentation see chapter 5.

PRACTISING YOUR DELIVERY

Rehearsing the presentation includes more than just going over it. To get the feel of the real thing you need to rehearse the entire presentation. Even though we have been doing presentations for years, we sometimes still rehearse in front of a mirror and always in front of each other. You get the opportunity to watch your facial expressions and work on them where necessary. Feedback is essential in your development as an excellent presenter. If you can present to the critical and often very frank audience of friends and family, you can present to any audience. Doing this will help you develop your own body language style and sort out any irritating mannerisms that you may have.

If possible, became familiar with the place in which you will present. Arrive early and walk around the the entire room including the presenting area. Stand at the podium, speak into the microphone. Walk around where the audience will be seated. Walk from where you will be seated to the place where you will be speaking. This will also help you to relax.

Remember: nothing can take the place of preparation.

Try using a tape recorder so that you can get an idea of the speed at which you talk and the number of 'uhm's' and 'aah's' in your presentation, which should be eliminated. It will also help you to work on projection of your voice, the pitch of your voice, rhythm and style.

When you rehearse, go through your entire presentation before making corrections. If you keep on stopping to make changes, you will never get to the end!

Have your preparation done well in advance so you can get a good night's rest before your presentation. There is nothing like fatigue to kill a good presentation.

Try to memorise the presentation like a parrot. Nerves and any distraction will make you fail badly if you are attempting to do this.

To project a professional image, you must know your presentation inside out. It's fine to depart occasionally from your written script when you present, but wandering presentations that lack focus or have long pauses to compose your thoughts are unacceptable.

This said, don't try to memorise the presentation parrot-fashion. Nerves and any distraction will make you fail badly. On the other hand, you should never be too dependent on your notes: rather work with keycards. Keycards are short summaries of phrases that will fit comfortably in your hand. Use as many as you like. Make sure that the print size is legible. Highlight only what you want to say. That will trigger the brain to stay on a certain route.

You could also fit your entire presentation on one mind-map. A useful presentation aid on your mind-map is a timeclock. For example, if you were to present a one-hour presentation, at the centre of your mind-map you include the following:

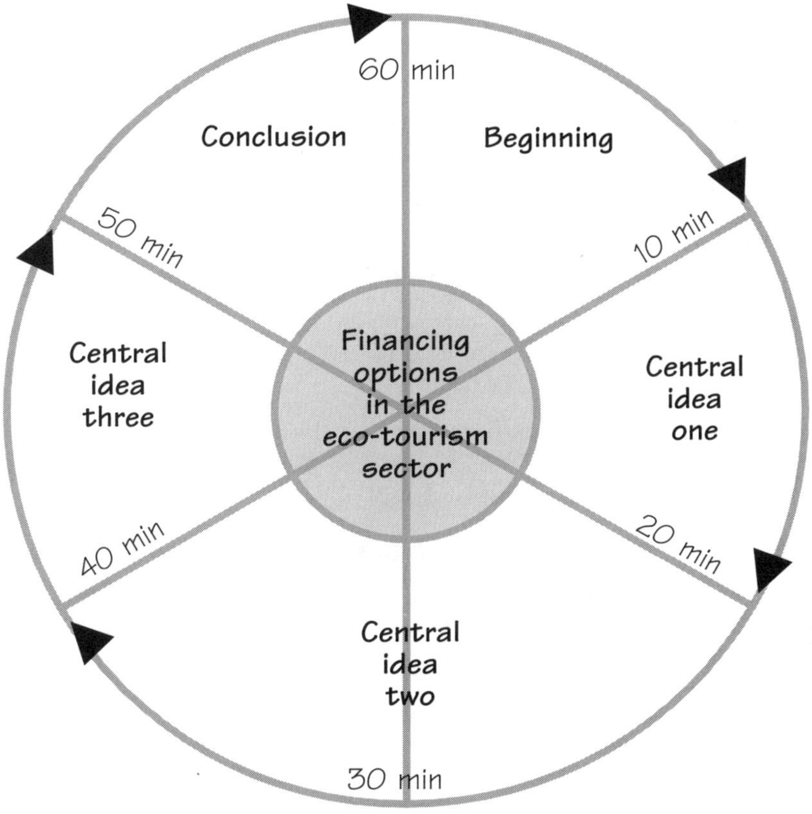

Use facts and figures to support what you say, but don't overkill.

Niki and Laura from The Communicator give these ten useful tips:

- Know who you are addressing, what the expectation is and how you hope to achieve it.

- Master your subject and speak with confidence.
- Prepare mind, body and voice before standing up and speaking out.
- Ensure that your introduction and conclusion have impact – your audience will always remember how you began and ended.
- Remain credible throughout – use only appropriate information, anecdotes and language, and don't try to impress the audience with irrelevant information.
- Let your body also do the talking with eye contact, facial expressions and gestures contributing to your platform presence.
- Keep a good grip on time – people's attention span drops after 40 minutes.
- Speak 'with' your audience, not 'at' them.
- Listen attentively and interact actively.
- Practise, practise, practise, you deserve to be heard!

The Grooming School feels that the following are important:

- Rehearse, rehearse, rehearse. Know exactly what you are going to say – never leave it up to chance!
- Make sure that you look your best: thinking about your unpolished shoes or the ladder in your stockings can easily distract you.
- Fill yourself with joyful thoughts before your presentation and (if you are a believer) then pray!
- Number the pages of your presentation.
- Never, ever have even a mouthful of sherry or anything alcoholic to calm your nerves.
- Don't be rushed – take time to gather your thoughts and focus.

If you don't feel comfortable with your presentation, you can still change it. You cannot do it when you stand in front of your audience. If you want to make changes, do so during the rehearsal stage. Take a short break, and practise again. We sometimes rehearse as many as ten times, depending on the complexity of our presentation.

Practice makes perfect, as they say.

Know your audience emotional speech and training.
Cookbook for nerves

GARNISHING 3

You are on your way to attend a presentation by a well-known public figure. As you drive, minding your own business, a huge luxury vehicle pulls up behind you, hoots for you to make way and, when you don't react fast enough, pushes you aggressively to the side of the road. You are naturally very upset about this road hog's conduct. Great is your surprise when you arrive at the venue and see this vehicle. You are even more surprised when you see the well-know speaker emerging from behind the steering wheel of this car.

You can make your first impression without knowing it. Beware! Before you have spoken your first word, you have already made your first impression by the way you are dressed and your body language.

CLOTHING

The way in which you are dressed is one of the most important contributors to the first impression that you create. The people in the audience attend to hear what you are about to say, they do not attend to be entertained by your appearance.

Unless the dress code is specifically stated in your invitation or determined by company policy, you can get away with any reasonable outfit.

The question of dress is a delicate balance between blending with the audience and your personal style. When dressing, you want to avoid funny-looking or distracting items, such as:

- hundreds of bangles dangling from both arms
- big earrings

- overly dramatic makeup
- tight fitting clothes which punctuate body unevenness
- a white belt around the waist
- wild and exotic hairstyles spreading over the face
- distracting fabrics, for example, stripes, checks, polka dots or
- glaringly bright colour schemes.

You can distract yourself and your audience with uncomfortable or bizarre outfits. If you constantly have to pull your skirt down, choke on a collar which is too tight or if you feel your feet going numb in a pair of designer shoes that you bought a number of sizes too small on a sale, you cannot possibly concentrate on the business at hand.

A 'reasonable' outfit is determined by the situation and your personal style. You do not want to blend in with the audience to the extent that you are not noticeable. On the other hand, you do not want to stand out like the proverbial sore thumb.

In essence, a useful approach to dress is that your clothes should be comfortable and appropriate to the occasion.

BODY LANGUAGE

If you understand body language, you will immediately have a greater understanding of your audience's wants and their needs.

If your body language gels with the content of your presentation, you have immediate credibility. If your presentation deals with the number of children that will be orphaned as a result of the spread of AIDS, you cannot present this with a smile on your face. Nobody will share your enthusiasm for the record profit level achieved by your department if you lean heavily and exhausted on the lectern, looking like a sundried tomato.

Each part of the body communicates something. When we ask workshop participants which part of the body they perceive as the most valuable communication mechanism, most people benefit from looking at someone's eyes.

Eye contact from you as presenter shows that you are interested and that you are listening. Effective eye contact gives credibility and creates openness. Eye contact must be direct – but keep in mind that this does not mean that you should stare at one person. When talking to the audience, your eye contact should move from person to person in a random way.

Eye contact should follow a pawpaw pattern of predictability, sweeping from side to side of the room, in a way that seems to be choreographed.

Use eye contact with your audience to determine whether they are interested and understand what you are saying. Members of the audience rolling their eyes may be an indication that they disagree with what you are saying. You can also gauge their enjoyment of your presentation with their degree of eye contact.

Apart from eye contact, you should also observe facial expressions. Frowns from the audience can indicate difficulty in understanding or difficulty in seeing visual material clearly. This could also mean that they are concentrating and paying attention to what you are saying, and that they are formulating questions that they may want answered.

If people in the audience are frowning, address the issue: do not ignore it and hope that it will go away. A first attempt to address the issue may be to interrupt your presentation by asking if what you have

said is clear, or whether you should clarify certain aspects. Ask the audience whether the visuals are clear: even if your oral presentation is clear, visuals that are difficult to see can be distracting. Remind the audience that you would appreciate and welcome questions and comments at the end of the presentation.

POSTURE, STANCE AND MOVEMENT

You want to create openness and a free flow of communication between yourself and the audience. This is created by standing comfortably and straight. The lectern is there to hold your notes, not you. Openness is further enhanced by relaxed arms and legs. Arms that are tightly crossed over the chest or tightly crossed legs indicate the closed or defensive attitude of the prickly-pear presenter.

Natural movement can promote openness between yourself and the audience. Take care that your movements do not become repetitive, such as an almost ritualistic pacing up and down. When you move on stage, take the layout of the stage into account: if the lighting in the venue is uneven, you may find yourself entering a no man's land of shadows on occasion.

Use directed and planned hand movements to emphasise certain points. Take care not to look like an officer directing traffic during rush hour with over-exaggerated or repetitive hand movements.

If you need to hold resource material in your hand, don't hold it squarely in front of you: rather position it slightly to your left or right in a lowered position in order not to obscure your face or chest area. This is vital.

COMMUNICATING YOUR UNDERSTANDING OF THE AUDIENCE

You can indirectly communicate to the audience that you have a real understanding of them by:

- mirroring (copycat) their body language
- appealing to their dominant senses.

Mirroring

If a member of the audience sits with arms crossed tightly, you could start your presentation by taking that same stance. In this manner, you are introducing mirroring into your conversation. As you gradually (and knowingly) relax, you will find that your audience will mirror your body language.

The mirroring technique can be used successfully with both small and large audiences. In a larger audience, you will find that groups of people sitting in close proximity will mirror each other's body language. In such a situation, you should focus on one group at a time, mirroring their body language.

Practise mirroring in social contexts until you feel comfortable with the concept. As time goes by, you will find yourself mirroring people and audiences without having to remind yourself to do so.

When you mirror an audience's body language, your audience feels that you understand them. You put your audience at ease by meeting them on their level and terms, which makes it easier to persuade them to join you and to open up to what you are talking about

Dominant senses

Another way in which you can communicate understanding to your audience is by appealing to their most dominant senses. This technique is based on the concepts of Neuro-Linguistic Programming, founded by Grinder and Bandler, scholars of linguistics, psychology and mathematics.

Close your eyes and visualise a Spanish dancer. What grabs your attention? Do you focus on:

- the dress, colour, physical features of the dancer, her hair or even her makeup
- the movement of the dress, her dancing
- the sound of the music, or sound of her castanets?

The first thing that you focussed on is an indication of your dominant sense.

If the dress, colour and visual components were your first focus points, your dominant sense is visual. You are a person who needs to see the picture of what you present and what is presented to you. For the benefit of visually dominant people in the audience you can make statements such as, 'Can you see the picture?', 'I see what you mean . . . ', 'I view this . . .', or 'Let's look at the following . . .'.

If the movement interested you, your dominant sense is kinaesthetic. You need to develop a gut feel of what you are busy with or presenting. Statements that will make sense to a kinaesthetically dominant person are 'I feel . . .', or 'My gut feel tells me . . .'.

If you focussed on the sound, your dominant sense is auditory. Things will sound good to you or not. Statements that will appeal to auditory dominant people are 'I hear what you say . . .', 'We heard the arguments . . .', 'Listen to the following . . .', or 'The following has a nice ring to it . . .'.

Your audience will probably consist of a mixed bag of predominantly visual, kinaesthetic and auditory people. Your presentation must address the predominant perspectives of all three of these groups, or mixtures of these groups.

You have to paint a picture, convey feeling, and make yourself heard.

STYLE

It is important that you develop a personal style of speaking. Most successful speakers have developed their own characteristic and unique pattern of presenting. Put your personal stamp on presentations through your rhythm and vocal nuances. Presenting is very personal. What works for others might not work for you.

You can develop that personal style in the following ways.

Use a conversational style

The use of mind-maps can assist you in developing this style of speaking. The reason for this is that you will only have keywords or phrases in front of you and this will enable you to speak with ease.

This style is similar to an ordinary conversation, but is adapted to the environment in which the presentation is delivered. This is nothing more than your day-to-day way of talking. You will sound more spontaneous, intimate and sincere. It's not that difficult either, because it's natural.

Express yourself in a frank way to your audience. Communication with your audience is more relaxed and believable if you speak spontaneously. Let your speech flow naturally and they will perceive you as sincere.

Gestures and movements

Never just stand up, straight as a ramrod, and shoot off your mouth at the audience. Use dynamic gestures and movement to enhance your presentation. The energy you put in will be the energy you get out of your audience. Move around on stage or in front of the audience, use your hands to emphasise and to appeal, use your eyes to show understanding and interest.

Expressing emotion

Our body language conveys our emotions in a very natural way. Emotion must be genuine. Don't force it on your audience. Don't act your emotions, as so many talk-show hosts (and their audiences) seem to do. If you are serious, show that you are serious; if you are amused, show that you are amused – but never try to be something that you are not. Remember: the more natural you stay, the easier it will be for your audience to believe you.

Keep it personal

Presenting, like public speaking, depends on personal style. You may get ideas from Larry King, Archbishop Tutu, Mr Mandela, but you are your own person. Do not try to be like them. Your style is unique to yourself and you should keep it like that.

Use vocal variety

For an effective presentation, vary the rate, loudness and pitch of your voice. Pay attention to rhythm, pauses, speed and the use of phrases. Your voice is your best tool. Use it wisely – more of this follows.

YOUR VOICE

Your voice is linked to the way you feel about yourself. It can indicate how relaxed and healthy you are. Your voice is part of your total image. It is unique to you in the same way as a fingerprint. Regard your voice as your second face.

We all probably dislike our own voice when we first hear it on a tape recording. However, do not be unduly upset: keep in mind that this has a distorting effect on how you hear your voice.

You don't need a radio announcer's voice to be an effective presenter. However, you must make sure that your voice can be heard and understood and that there is tonal variety.

If you speak too softly, the audience will give up straining to hear. Remember, you may have to compete with noises from outside, latecomers, the rattle of china and cutlery, airconditioning and people sneezing and coughing.

The secret of voice projection is to use your breath to support your voice as you speak from your stomach. If you exert pressure on your throat muscles to speak louder, your voice will sound strained and you will end up with a sore throat.

To project your voice, you need lots of breath. Practise as though projecting your voice to the back of the State Theatre. You should be able to hear the difference as you use more air to carry your voice further.

Don't let your voice drop at the end of a sentence, but maintain the same volume right to the final full stop.

A lot of people speak with their teeth pressed together. Say the alphabet out loud, opening your mouth as wide as possible. This will help you with clarity. Clarity and good diction do not mean changing your accent or personality, but do mean pronouncing every letter and sound in order to minimise the risk of being misunderstood.

Many pitfalls in presenting arise because people don't trust their breath to provide power and clarity and so they overcompensate with other parts of their bodies. Exercise to control your breath and speech. Poor breath control is characterised by sharp, short intakes of breath and a feeling of panic and breathlessness. You will find that you have no control over your voice projection and that there is excessive and unnecessary movement in your shoulders and chest on inhaling. This will influence the effect of your presentation. If you feel that you are losing control over your breathing, you will soon feel that you are losing control of the entire presentation.

You should also aim to add tonal variety to your voice. Even if the content of your presentation is stimulating, you will not have credibility and you won't keep your audience's attention if your voice sounds unenthusiastic

Play around with volume. Stress an important point by saying it louder, but without shouting it at the audience. Emphasise the right words at the right time.

People who are nervous tend to speak faster. Try to control the speed at which you speak. The content of your presentation will also determine this: you may want to speak slightly slower when you want to emphasise a point. Vary your pace. Speak slower to set a particular mood and faster to create excitement.

Use pitch to underline something in your presentation. The lower you speak, the louder your voice will be and the slower you will talk.

Time yourself: how many words do you speak in a minute? Most people speak about 150 words a minute in public.

Emphasis: Emphasise the right words at the right time.

Pause: Pauses are very effective to create tension, suspense and expectation, and to provoke thought.

Remember: quality of voice gives you freedom of speech.

Here are a few more pointers from The Communicator to help you along the way:

- Avoid stop-gap phrases such as 'OK', 'ja', 'you know...' or 'Uh'.
- Pause when you want to draw the audience's attention to a particular point.
- Always use a rich, resonant voice and avoid sounding flat, harsh, too soft or too loud.
- Concentrate on a clear tone and speak with energy.
- Vary the pitch, pace, volume and rhythm at which you speak.

- Grasp the audience's attention by increasing volume when making an important point.
- Focus on correct breathing and ensure that you end each sentence on a strong note.
- Give full value to vowel and consonant sounds in order to articulate each sentence correctly.
- Use inflection – allow your voice to rise when asking questions and fall when making statements.

Yolisa Dalamba from Across Borders Arts Education suggests these exercises for your voice:

- **Colouring your presentation**
  You need a tape recorder. Tape your presentation when reading it aloud. Do it again, but apply different rhythms to it. Play with the pauses between sections. If you feel comfortable with this, do it again, but apply different emotions through pauses, melodiousness and accents to make it more interesting. Listen to how it changed and apply what you feel comfortable with.
- **Sing your presentation**
  Think of two songs that have different rhythms and sing your presentation to their rhythm. Listen to how it changed and apply what you feel comfortable with.
- **Body speech**
  You need a friend for this exercise. Try to communicate your presentation only using physical gestures, then repeat the presentation using gibberish (sounds) and see if you are still understood. Use the gestures you feel improve your presentation and apply them.

It's not always what you say, but how you say it!

USE SPACE EFFECTIVELY

The space between you and the members of the audience will contribute to the atmosphere that you create. Can you remember the first time that you watched a news programme on e-tv? Seeing the presenters close by, without a desk in front of them, certainly captures your attention. In a similar way you can use the concept of space to work for you during a presentation.

Some books on presentation give you precise measurements of how many metres and centimetres you are supposed to be from your audience. Our approach is more relaxed. You will immediately sense whether you or the members of the audience are comfortable or uncomfortable with the space between you and them.

If you feel like a survivor of a shipwreck who is washed ashore on a deserted island and trying desperately to attract the attention of ships on the horizon, you are too far from the audience. Alternatively, if your audience should begin to twitch, become tense and adopt closed body language, it is time to move a step or two backwards. You don't want to make the audience feel wrapped up and compressed in a vacuum pack.

React to your feelings of closeness to and distance from your audience.

Remove objects such as stands and tables that you feel would create distance between yourself and your audience. However, if it gives you a greater feeling of security and self-confidence, do not hesitate to stand behind a table or a chair. Try to avoid a situation where it is difficult to make eye contact with the audience because you are on a stage that is too high or too far from them.

The more accurate your estimate of closeness and distance, the more open you will seem to the audience.

PSYCHOBABBLE 4

In describing the reasonable man, Judge Holmes said: 'One does not expect from the reasonable man any extremes such as Solomonic wisdom, prophetic foresight, chameleonic caution, headlong haste, nervous timidity, or the trained reflexes of a racing driver. In short, a reasonable man treads life's pathway with moderation and prudent common sense.' We would like to add to this that any reasonable person would show significant levels of stress when faced with delivering a presentation. Such high stress levels can result in a fruit salad of idiotic statements, tunnel vision, clumsiness, scattered reason, the courage and arrogance of ignorance, and the exposure of foolish flair.

Delivering a presentation may not be the nightmare experience described above, but we are still looking for the reasonable person who can describe their first presentation as the most relaxing experience they have ever had.

We all become stressed when we present (even the professionals). We all need to stress when we present.

THE NEED FOR STRESS

Stress is as synonymous with presentation as opening your mouth and talking. We all experience stress. The good news is that we are all supposed to experience it. We need stress to deliver a good performance.

Have you ever experienced the nerve-racking feeling when a body part starts twitching involuntarily and uncontrollably? We had that experience when, during a radio talk-show, a steady hand needed to be placed on a knee to eliminate the sound of it knocking against the table. If the distracting nature of too much stress can be limited, this new level of stress might be exactly what is needed for that extra *oomph* in your performance.

Performance and stress are directly linked. John Gribbin called this the Goldilocks effect. Goldilocks tested the chairs, porridge and beds until she found those that were just right. You need to do the same with your stress levels. Too little stress will detract from your ability to perform and leave you with a lukewarm, flat performance. Too much stress will leave you wound up so tight that all systems (such as memory) will close down on you and leave you unable to do what you want to do.

We all know the tell-tale signs of too much stress: sweaty palms, neck spasms, loss of voice, shortness of breath, diarrhoea, dry mouth, palpitations, perspiration, butterflies and those uncontrollable shakes.

During a trial in the High Court, an officer from the Department of Correctional Services testified on the functioning of the Parole Board. The judge gave him a hard time, shouting at him several times. This resulted in the official becoming even more nervous and anxious. The judge asked him to explain the composition of the Parole Board. In a shaky voice, the official mentioned a number of people on this board, including correctional supervision staff and criminal professors. Surely this nervous witness was in no state to appreciate his real contribution to the proceedings! For those unfamiliar with the justice system, the official intended to refer to professors in criminology and not to professors who had committed crimes! We can all think of times when we blurted out some inappropriate comment as a result of high levels of anxiety.

It does not matter how well prepared you are, you will still experience some of the signs of nervousness. See them for what they are. Reassure yourself that everybody goes through this, that you are quite normal, and that you need it.

> *What is going on inside does not necessarily reflect what you look like on the outside. So although you may feel extremely anxious, your audience might not even notice.*

There are a number of techniques that you can use to control stress before your presentation.

Breathing techniques

When you are under stress, your breathing pattern becomes more erratic. When people feel pressured, they tend to hyperventilate. That numbness in the face or pins and needles in you ice-cold fingertips is the unpleasant result of hyperventilation. This is the time to resort to a breathing technique.

- Look in the mirror and take a deep breath until your shoulders and chest rise.
- Lie on your back on the floor. Relax. Bend your knees so that your feet are flat on the floor. Put a cushion under your head to follow the natural curve of your spine. Place one hand flat on the centre of your stomach and yawn out. Sigh in and yawn out. Sense that the sighs and the yawns are coming from your stomach and that your stomach is collapsing as you let sound out.
- Still on the floor, have a good belly laugh. There will be some movement on the stomach. In the same position breathe in,

feeling the stomach rise and sensing it fall as you gently breathe out.

- Keep one hand on your stomach. Breathe easily and say your name as you breathe out.
- Sit up. If your chest begins to rise then place your hand on it to remind you to relax. Close your eyes and repeat steps 1 to 3.
- Stand up and do this exercise five times while standing. Check for physical tension. Make sure that your shoulders are relaxed and dropped and that your chest has not risen.

Note: If you feel dizzy at any time during this exercise, stop. It is likely that you have increased your oxygen intake too much and surprised your brain.

Another breathing exercise is to breathe deeply in and out. Control your breath so that it takes you three seconds to breathe out. If you have some privacy, breathe in loudly and blow the air out through your lips. If you do not have the benefit of privacy, just breathe in and out. Every time you inhale, tell yourself that you are breathing relaxation; every time that you exhale, tell yourself that you are breathing out tension. Pace your breathing while repeating 'relaxation in – tension out – relaxation in – tension out'. Continue this exercise for as long as you feel it is needed.

Remember: you do not need to and do not want to feel absolutely relaxed. If you still have some butterflies left after doing the exercise, it is fine, because you need that to perform optimally. As somebody once said, you do not want to get rid of your butterflies, you want to teach them to fly in formation.

Backtrack in history

Take a moment to think back on what you consider your most successful talk or presentation. If you have never presented, think of a conversation with friends where you took centre stage.

Do you remember how you felt? Now write down some of those emotions.

1 ....

2 ....

3 ....

4 ....

Now start to feel those emotions exactly as you felt them that day. Close your eyes, see yourself talking and recreate those feelings of confidence, excitement, eagerness to communicate or any other emotion that you felt. Use this backtracking exercise for its calming effect before a presentation.

Find the image

Prepare this exercise at home and then use it when you are waiting to deliver your talk or presentation.

Think of a metaphor that currently describes you as a presenter. Examples of such metaphors could be:

- I am a rocket on a launch pad that is not quite ready for lift off.
- I am a fish in an empty pond.
- I am a plum picked too soon.
- I am a computer ready for use but waiting for the correct instructions.

Now think of a metaphor that describes you as the presenter you want to be. Examples of such metaphors could be:

- I am an inspired conductor, conducting the orchestra in playing my favourite piece of music.
- I am an athlete winning gold at the Olympic Games.
- I am a fruit salad waiting in the crystal bowl for the cream on top.
- I am an archer aiming the arrow and hitting the bull's eye.

My old metaphor is:

....

My new metaphor is:

....

This new metaphor is the image that you carry in your mind to the presentation. We learn better and more by using images as opposed to using facts and behavioural routines. While you are waiting to give your presentation, run this new image through your mind, seeing yourself acting and reacting in the way you want to.

Rapid relaxation technique

The extent to which you can use this technique will be determined by the privacy you have. The public toilet at the venue can give you some privacy. Contract all the muscles in your face for seven seconds and then relax for three seconds. Repeat this twice. Squeeze the muscles in your face as if it is an orange from which you want to extract the last drop of juice. For obvious reasons, this part of the exercise should be omitted if you have no privacy.

Contract all the muscles in your upper body for about seven seconds and relax for about three seconds. Repeat this twice. Now contract all the muscles in the lower part of your body for about seven seconds and relax for about three seconds. Repeat this twice. Now contract all the muscles in your entire body for about seven seconds and relax for about three seconds. Repeat this twice. After completing these rapid relaxation exercises, you can continue with the breathing techniques described earlier.

How to deal with presentation stress and panic

You have worked so hard on your presentation that you should be entitled simply to enjoy it. During a presentation the world around you can become so small that your existence is focussed only on this presentation at this moment. Such a situation can create stress and tension.

Stress and even panic can set in at any time during the presentation. How do you prevent such a situation? What can you do when you experience the signs of stress, such as shaking hands, a loss of breath or having no idea what you have said or what you are supposed to say next?

There are many things that you can do to remove the immediate pressure from yourself:

- Widen your perspective, such as by scanning the room and taking in what you see.
- Breathe.
- Engage in natural movements: start to walk, take a sip of water, or stretch your arms.
- Switch to your visual aids. If you feel all the focus and pressure are on you, turn to your visual aids to shift the attention to a transparency or a slide. You can ask the audience to study this for a moment, or to discuss a point briefly with the person next to them. Move back and look at your visual aid. These actions will give you those few seconds that you need to regain your composure, to organise your thoughts and to focus.
- Anchor yourself until you feel that you have stabilised. There are many ways of anchoring. Physically you can anchor yourself by standing with your feet hip-width apart, solidly planted on the ball of the foot, with your feet facing the front, your body tilted slightly forward and your shoulders relaxed. This will stabilise your posture, which in turn will improve your breathing and projection of your voice. If you have a written text, you can anchor yourself by reading from the text. Another way of anchoring yourself is to refer to your mind-map or other resource notes, again breathing deeply, slowly and rhythmically. If you take a moment or two to do so, nobody will notice.

SELF-CONFIDENCE

Most people that we consult in workshops and in other situations see self-confidence as illusive.

Every day is different

The first aspect that we want to emphasise is that nobody experiences the same levels of confidence every day. There are days when you feel so confident that you can conquer the world. But then there are days when you lack self-confidence so much that you feel like driving to work on the back seat of your own car! This lack of self-confidence can exist either because of a valid reason, or because of something entirely unfounded.

We all know those days when you wake up and stare in the mirror with horror at the person who stares back at you. Your mind starts to race from one catastrophic thought to the next and before you know it you have convinced yourself that you will never be able to deliver a presentation that day.

The best way to counteract those moments of low self-confidence is to get your mind on a different track or to change gears mentally. Think of things that you find pleasant, things that elicit feelings of success and inner comfort. Take your mind off yourself and your own anxieties and start following different thoughts. Become active: sitting and pondering on these negative feelings will only make matters worse.

How serious is the problem?

If you feel that the problem is deeper than temporary flashes of low self-confidence, you have a few options. If the problem is so serious that it impacts on your daily functioning, social life and performance at work, it would be beneficial to consult a psychotherapist or a medical practitioner.

First-time-around confidence

The first time around, you only want to survive the presentation. This does not necessarily mean that you will have fun or think that you were terrific in giving this presentation. The first time around, you are usually very critical of your performance. Have patience. It may be a cliché, but you first have to crawl before you can walk.

Ask for feedback – it is a helpful way to evaluate your presentation.

Feedback is a useful tool in improving your skills: it is not intended as a personal attack or personal criticism. Don't focus on what went wrong the first time or view your mistakes as an inability to be a successful presenter. Rather learn from the feedback and start to plan how you can address these aspects in your next presentation. After surviving the first few presentations you can start to experiment.

Improve your self-confidence

What obstacles prevent you from being confident?

You first have to establish what obstacle are interfering with your self-confidence before you can actively start to address them.

Different people experience different obstacles. Some people are perfectionists and want to do things perfectly the first time around. They do not allow themselves the opportunity to make mistakes and to learn from these mistakes. This results in them either not trying because of the fear of failure, or being so hard and critical on themselves that they don't enjoy their own presentations.

Some people are sensitive about a physical attribute, such as their weight, facial features or bad teeth. Others compare themselves to professional presenters or politicians and then tell themselves that they will never be able to speak like Martin Luther King or Tony Blair, and so they will never be able to deliver a presentation.

Now write down the obstacles you have identified that destroy your self-confidence.

1 ....

2 ....

3 ....

4 ....

5 ....

Are these obstacles

- something that you can change? Apart from plastic surgery, there is nothing you can do about your physical features. You probably feel that they are very noticeable, but the question remains whether anybody else notices!
- your problem or other people's problem? You sit and think for hours what other people will say about you. That is their problem and not yours: never allow other people to erode your self-confidence.
- something you want to do something about? If your weight bothers you, you can worry about it or you can do something about it. In general, if you are pear-shaped, you are pear-shaped; and if you are apple-shaped, you are apple-shaped.

If you develop a preoccupation with the problem and turn this into your main focus, you will erode your own self-confidence.

Now write down how you would act differently if you were confident within yourself.

1 ....

2 ....

3 ....

4 ....

5 ....

Now write down which of these actions you can start with immediately.

1 ....

2 ....

3 ....

Lastly, consider what emotions you will experience if you are confident within yourself.

1 ....

2 ....

Remember: confidence grows and develops over time.

Develop stamina in presentation self-confidence

You can develop stamina in self-confidence in the same manner as you can develop stamina in running or cycling. The best way to develop stamina is to present. Present. Present. Present.

We don't feel the same levels of self-confidence every day.

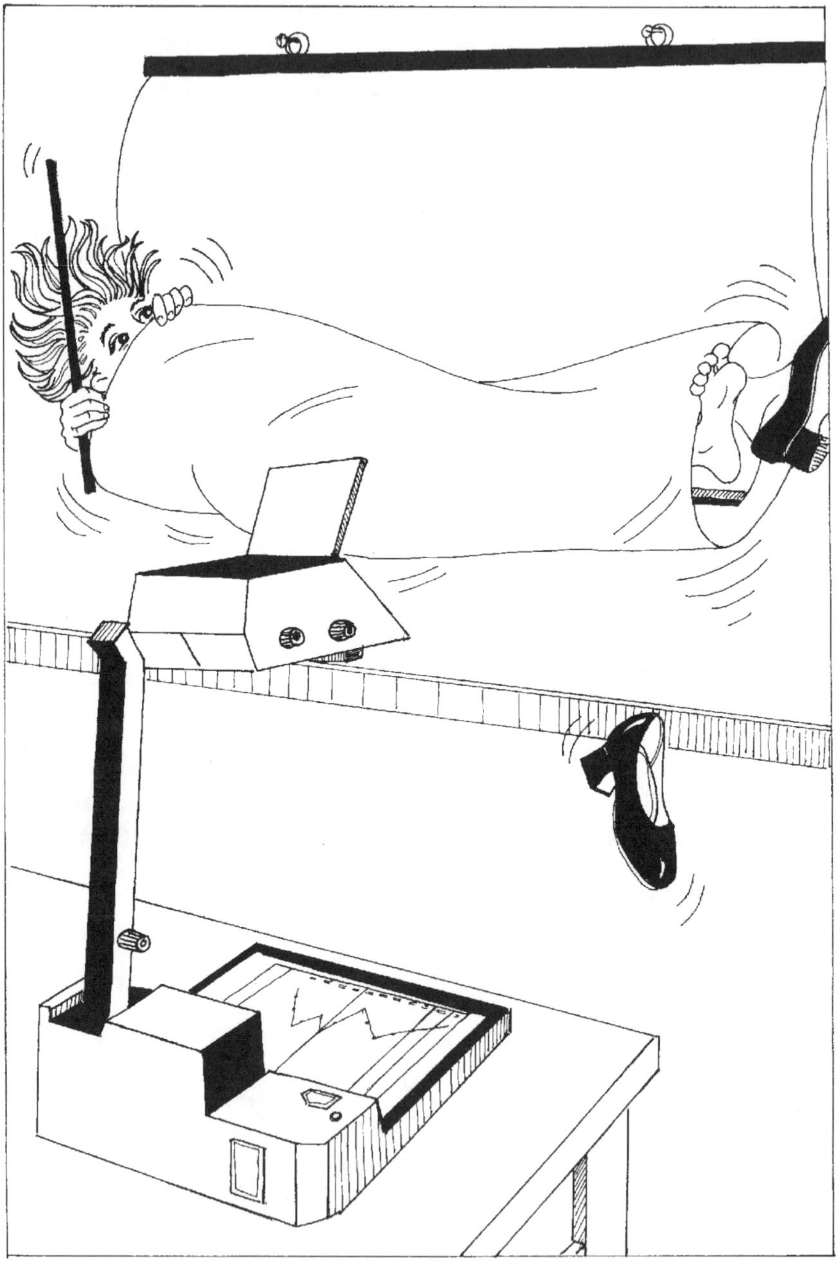

HOW TO USE THE FRUIT SHAKER, AND OTHER TOOLS 5

Even the magician Houdini used technology to improve his shows. Just after radios became popular, he started using them as part of his act. He would show the audience a big radio, standing on a table, with nothing inside. He would then cover it with a large golden cloth. He would call out the name of the radio station in that region and his assistant, Miss Young, would jump out of the radio and dance to some background music. Houdini was known as someone who admitted that technology could only make you look better in front of the audience.

As we are entering a new millennium, most of us have access to a laptop computer and/or projector. In the last couple of years, presentation products have made tremendous strides. Presentation products have evolved as much in the past two years as computers have done in the last five.

Great news, certainly, yet now everyone expects more of you and your presentation. If you want to play the game of professional presentation, get on board or get out of the game!

In the past, presentation material was limited to the typical overhead and separate video presentations. This created a somewhat technical dilemma for the presenter.

Today we have the convenience of multimedia and other techno wonders, which means that we can produce interactive presentations.

The most important reason for using visual aids is to involve the senses of your audience. Research has shown that the more senses are used during the learning process, the better the retention of the message.

The aids currently available help make contact with your audience and ensure that your presentation is successful. This is mainly because visual aids help you enhance the audience's understanding of the topic and increase the entertainment value of your presentation. They will also help you to add authenticity and variety, to give your presentation extra impact and *woema*.

For any visual aid to be effective, you must be experienced in using it. Nothing is as distracting as visuals that do not make sense or do not fit your verbal presentation.

There is nothing worse than the presenter who does not know how to get the focus right or which buttons to push to get the equipment working properly.

Plan the placing of the visual prior to your presentation. You should know exactly where and when you want to show your audience something. Your verbal presentation should be complemented by your visuals.

An executive once decided to go for broke and used automotion with PowerPoint for his presentation. The only problem was that he had the images moving along every three seconds, which left the audience breathless and eyesore, trying to read what was flashing past them. Needless to say, the entire visual presentation carried on like this, nonstop for five minutes. Embarrassed, the executive could just manage a half-witted: 'I'm still of the old school, I'm more used to slides.' (To add insult to injury, he represents a hi-tech video company!)

Such a situation need not turn into a total disaster – provided you keep your presence of mind and improvise. After all, nobody knows that this was not part of plan A. In a situation like the above, take control, move to plan B and tell your audience: 'We'll quickly run through the main points of this presentation and then I will explain the finer details of this solution to you.' Having said this, you simply read the points as they appear on the screen. When you have exhausted plan B – and your face should by now have returned to its natural colour – you can go back to plan A.

> *A visual aid is only as good as its user's ability to employ it.*

It is also vital that you make sure that all electronic equipment works beforehand, and that you know where to switch everything on. We cannot blame the Japanese electronics industry for everything! Technology is great, but it depends on basics, like power. It can be the nightmare of nightmares if your equipment fails to work.

Practise how to use your equipment, where to put it in the room (make sure everyone can see it), where you should stand and when to use your visual aid. Do not fall in the same trap as a certain presenter: he had positioned himself in front of a big screen with the blue projection light on his face during his whole presentation. What a case of presenting and talking until 'blue in the face'!

While effective presenting does not require visual aids, a few well-placed visuals can add a significant amount of clarity and impact. They will certainly spice up your presentation. But don't be fooled: visuals with little substance and little to contribute can destroy an otherwise well-structured and excellently delivered presentation. For visual aids to have any major effect, they must support the structure of a well-developed presentation. Visual aids are just that: aids; they are not the presentation.

STATIC AIDS

Static visual aids include posters, slides, overhead transparencies and drawings.

Although less popular now than they once were, they are still very effective for enhancing a presentation and for use as back-ups. Depending on your audience and the set-up of the venue, you may have no other choice than to use static visual aids. Although these aids may not have quite the attention-getting potential as dynamic visual aids, they can still be very effective. They are also easier to prepare and use.

The well-known speaker Edward de Bono exploits the full potential of static aids and his presentations are lively, fun and conversational. He places a continuous transparency sheet (about four meters long) over pre-prepared transparencies and writes on the continuous transparency as he goes. This means that he can further illustrate the pre-prepared transparencies without destroying the original. If you want to do this, you have to be very comfortable with using overhead projectors.

When preparing slides, avoid yellow and red: these colours are difficult to see and tire the eye. Also avoid a combination of red and green: most people who are colour blind are unable to distinguish between these colours and the purpose of your visual aid will be lost.

DYNAMIC VISUAL AIDS

Dynamic visual aids include video, audio, computer graphics, and actual moving objects. Presentations can be on the perfect platform: CD-ROM, which can hold large files of information. You could amaze your audience at the click of a button.

HOW TO USE THE FRUIT SHAKER

YOONEEK Interactive gives the following advice:

More and more businesses recognise that electronic brochuring (CD-ROMs) are becoming powerful business tools. Businesses are finding electronic brochuring a necessity for presentation purposes; and the CD contains a slide show with or without speaker support. A range of languages can be available to your viewers. Video can be part of the CD-ROM, either compressing to AVI or a new improved technology, MPEG2, that plays out 25 frames per second.

Some of the benefits of multimedia are:

- Improved aesthetic quality
- Its ability to make use of a wide range of source material from corporate archives
- Better impact on an audience
- Improved retention of information
- Greater flexibility both for the presenter and producer
- Multiple delivery platforms, e.g. CD-ROM, laptop, PC and Internet.

Multimedia corporate presentations using Internet developments can be described as the combination of text, graphics, animation, video and sound played on a single digital platform. Multimedia is fast replacing traditional overheads, slides and linear video as the technology of choice for corporate presentations and marketing communication.

The use of any technology without practising or understanding it could lead to major embarrassment.

Your choice of dynamic visual aids should depend on the time you have available for the presentation, the venue, your personality, and the time you need to create them and practise with them. Always remember that a simple visual aid, used well, is much more effective than a complex one, used poorly.

Technology can ruin your presentation if you don't use it correctly: ask the presenter who had to deliver a presentation with the multimedia projector out of focus and the bottom part of the slide show cut off. Moreover, the venue had no screen and he had to use a whiteboard covered with permanent marker.

DOS AND DON'TS

- Visuals should add to the presentation, not detract from it.
- Your visuals must be clearly visible and understandable to the entire audience.
- Use a simple and large size for easy reading.
- Avoid distributing objects to the audience while you are speaking.
- Practise using your visuals well ahead of time in order to integrate them smoothly into your performance.
- Expect the unexpected: have back-ups.
- Visuals can only add to the value of a presentation, they cannot rescue a poorly developed presentation.
- Speak to your audience, not your visual aids.
- Keep it short and simple.
- Use the visuals only to enhance what you are saying, not to repeat all the information. Trust us, the members of the audience don't want to read essays.
- People don't want to follow the bouncing balls.
- Use charts and graphs for statistics.
- Don't display anything until you are ready to use it.
- Don't stand in front of your visuals; the audience will try to look past (and through) you rather than pay attention to what you are saying.

- When referring to something on the visual aid, point to it: don't leave your audience searching.
- Check your use of colour.

It is impossible to explain here how to operate all presentation software. Use the websites below for more information about presentation software:

HELPFUL WEBSITES

ASAP Wordpower
http://www.spco.com/
ASAP has been cited by multimedia reviewers as a very good package for preparing a slide show quickly. The ASAP Web Show and Active Presenter are plug-ins to use with Netscape or as helpers for the Microsoft Internet Explorer to view ASAP pages on the Web.

Astound
http://www.astoundinc.com
Astound is one of the most useful software packages for creating presentations. Astound Webeast allows you to create your own channels for using push technology to interact with visitors to your website without special server software.

Corel Presentations 8
http://www.corel.com/products/wordperfect/cp8/index.htm
It incorporates the Show-all feature for displaying slides on a Web page.

Harvard Graphics
http://www.spco.com/PRODUCTS/HARVMAIN>HTM
One of the first programs for creating visual aids, it is still useful for creating slide shows.

Lotus
http://www2.lotus.com/freelance.nsf
Freelance is one of the components of the Lotus SmartSuite. It also features the WebScreen ShowPlayer.

Microsoft PowerPoint
http://www.microsoft.com/products/prodref/127ov.htm

Added creations
http://metacreations.com.products
With this you'll be able to give PowerPoint some pizzazz.

Compare
http://www.threedgraphics.com

Visual Thunder
http://www.muddyshoes.com

Microsoft
http://www.microsoft.com/msdownload
For users of Windows, this is a great source for downloading free software. A number of multimedia tools used for Web viewing are available, including the Microsoft Internet Explorer, the PowerPoint Animation viewer, the PowerPoint Viewer, Active X Controls, and Microsoft's VRML Viewer.

Netscape
http://home.netscape.com
Download the latest version of Netscape, one of the premier Web browsers.

Winfo
http://www.winmag.com/scripts/winfo.pl
Use this page provided by *Windows Magazine* to search for multimedia plug-ins for your browser. You can also find product reviews that Windows has done.

Webmonkey search for browsers
http://www.hotwired.com/webmonkey/browserkit
This is a search tool on HotWired that you can use to identify the platform and type of capabilities you want your browser to achieve.

Adobe Acrobat
http://www.adobe.com/prodindex/acrobat/main.html
This cross-platform allows you to create .pdf (portable document format) documents.

Adobe Acrobat
http://www.adobe.com/proddindex/acrobat/main..html
Download the free Acrobat reader to view .pdf documents on screen as they would appear in print (including graphics, tables and equations) and to print out a copy on your own printer.

Adobe PhotoShop
http://ww.adobe.com
Adobe's PhotoShop is one of the best programs for manipulating graphic images.

DSP Group
http://www.dspg.com/dspg.htm
Put sound files on your page compressed with True Speech. True Speech functionality is already built into Windows 95. But if you use another platform, use this site to download the software for converting (if need be) files to True Speech.

Gif Animation on the WWW
http://members.aol.com/royale/gifanim.htm
This online tutorial is useful for creating animated gif images.

HotWired
http://www.hotwired.com/webmonkey/toolbox/
Use some of the tools recommended by HotWired. Links for downloading are also provided.

JASC
http://www.jasc.com/index.html
JASC is the producer of Paint Shop Pro, one of the most versatile graphic programs for manipulating bitmap images.

HotBot
http://www.hotbot.com/
Click on 'media type' on HotBot's search page and you can designate the type of file that you are looking for. One set of radio boxes lets you choose a type of medium and another input form allows you to type in the extension of the file type.

Lycos Pictures and Sounds
http://www.lycos.com/lycosmedia.html
Try out this function of Lycos to locate images and sound files that it has indexed.

World Wide Web Virtual Library for Audit
http://www.comlab.ox.ac.uk/archive/audio.html
This WWW3 library provides links to live radio programming around the world. This site also has some useful links for finding sound archives, Usenet groups dealing with audio, and locating software for sound. Listen to it all . . . from bird songs in the Australian Botanical Gardens to tunes from Rock 'n Roll's Hall of Fame.

Downtown.com
htttp://www.presentation.com
To shop around, and to make your life more fun, to see what's on and what's not in the techno world. You will find anything from audio equipment to slide shows, projectors, software and books. You just may want to start your presentation here!

While not crucial to the success of your presentation, visual aids used effectively often mean the difference between a good presentation and a great presentation.

IT'S MUNCHTIME, FOLKS 6

Albert Einstein was once asked to deliver a presentation at Harvard University. When it was his turn to present, he walked up to the podium and said, 'I really have nothing to say,' and walked off. The audience stared at him in disbelief. He returned to podium and said, 'When I have something to say, I promise I'll come back.'

We don't recommend this to the first-time presenter!

After all your hard work, you have in hand the masterpiece of masterpieces. It represents months of research, audience analysis, and hours of preparation. Your moment of truth has arrived when all your hard work comes to fruition: the day when you step onto the podium and deliver your presentation.

Your presentation is an advertisement of your ideas. Shout it out loud!

Address your audience: 'you' is a very powerful word. It is direct and strong. It shows that you are not scared to talk to your audience.

Well, before you do this, you have to check a few things first:

- You have rehearsed your presentation beforehand. Rehearse one more time, even if it means doing it in front of faithful Fido.
- Be on time. Again make sure where, when and at what time the presentation is to be. Rather be early than late. This will give you time to relax.
- Have all your material available. Make sure that you have all the equipment you require.
- Have back-ups. Technology is great but if it doesn't work, it's a disaster. Do you have a plan B in the event of a power failure?

- If you have prepared handouts, make sure you have them readily available.
- Check that your equipment is connected and that it is set up correctly.
- Make sure that your keycards, mind-maps or other sources are on hand.
- Never do any presentation without on-site technical support. Know who to call and where to find them.
- Make a note of the contact number of the organiser.
- Make sure that you know your way to the venue and that it is easily accessible.

You are at the venue, well prepared, neatly dressed, with everything that you need on hand. All that is left now is to do it. Don't blow it by ignoring important basic rules.

- You know what you want to say – so say it! Jump in and go for it.
- Don't apologise for being nervous. It is normal to be nervous. This does not mean that you have to focus any attention on it.
- Never start with something negative. Never apologise for anything at the beginning. This is the first thing your audience will hear and the first thing that they will remember.
- Keep the presentation focussed on the message. Don't get carried away with all sorts of razzle-dazzle.
- Don't start presenting before you are properly situated in front of your audience. They need some time to size you up and you need time to take a good breath.
- Be in control of your audience; don't let them control you. Use your knowledge of body language. Look at your audience, observe them, be open, and don't hide from them. Let them know you are there. You want to achieve big things with your audience. You also want them to understand your message. It is not important whether they agree with you or not, as long as they get your message.
- Don't memorise your presentation. Stress may cause you to have a blank moment. However, you should know your presentation well

enough only to have to glance at your reference material here and there: do not read from it.

- Keep it short and simple. Just because the big moment has arrived, it does not mean that you should veer from your original plans.
- Be conscious of distractions such as cellphones ringing, people walking in late, echoes on the microphone. Do something about these distractions if you can.
- If you make a mistake, don't focus all the attention on that. Carry on and correct it gradually. Don't ignore mistakes, live with them.
- You have planned for questions: address questions and concerns as they come up.
- Pace yourself – don't go too fast or too slow.
- Be flexible. If someone passes out in the audience, show compassion, stay in control. At that stage, time is not everything.
- When doing a business presentation, it makes sense to give the audience handouts at the start of the presentation. However, use your discretion in deciding when the audience should have their handouts. You don't want the audience to page through during your presentation: quickly run through the handout before discussing it fully.

Avoid the following before you speak. They might have a negative effect on you:

- iced water (your voice works with a muscle: don't freeze it before the time)
- fizzy cold drinks (you don't want to burp at the audience, now do you?)
- lemon or sour drinks (they have a squeaky effect on the muscle)
- coffee or milk (they tend to thicken the saliva and you may just splatter all over the place).

Make sure not to eat 'easy to grow on your smile' food, like spinach.

Rather have tea without milk. Try herbal teas. Camomile tea has a soothing effect.

However, even though you are nervous, eat something light before a presentation, otherwise you may become dizzy from a drop in your blood-sugar level. We know that we said start with something dramatic, but fainting . . . . Avoid eating spicy food: you can imagine what can go wrong with this!

You have followed all the dos and don'ts. You are in front of your audience. Before you do anything else, you have to establish your credibility and competence with the audience.

Smell like a perfume factory or like a bath-less creature. You want your audience to smell you before seeing you!

ESTABLISHING CREDIBILITY AND COMPETENCE

The degree to which the audience *perceives* you as knowledgeable about the topic on the basis of your education, professional expertise and personal experience is known as your credibility or competence. Create the perception of competence by explicitly stating how you have developed your knowledge to speak on the subject. This will also depend on how much members of your audience know about the subject and how much they agree or disagree with you.

In general, the greater the degree of resistance from your audience, the more you will have to provide credible evidence of your expertise. This does not mean that you have to wave your academic certificates around. Rather make sure that the person who introduces you has an abbreviated, but comprehensive, CV available to rely on. But beware: a poor presentation can undermine your credibility, no matter your credentials.

The audience will make value judgements about your character and trustworthiness. These are perceptions about your moral virtues. It is important to bring across your message in the most reliable and consistent manner possible, without resorting to banalities or vulgarities.

The topic of your presentation can affect the audience's perception, especially when you are dealing with controversial value-related issues, such as abortion, the death penalty, animal rights and politically incorrect topics. A sensitive approach towards personal, cultural and community values will not only gain the audience's goodwill and respect, but will also build your character as a presenter.

HANDLING DIFFICULT SITUATIONS

Things are not going according to plan

You were told that you would have an hour for your presentation. The other presenters did not stick to the time limit and as you walk to the lectern, the chairperson casually informs you that, due to time constraints, you will have only thirty minutes. What now?

Apologise and make excuses. Use the half an hour of your already cut time to explain your predicament.

Stick to the points of your central message. Don't try to adapt your presentation. Present your introduction and conclusion in their entirety. If you have to cut part of your presentation, cut the body, but make sure that you put the main points of your central message across.

Never apologise. Don't make excuses.

People are not listening

Jump to conclusions that you are a bad and ineffective presenter who cannot even engage an audience.

Rather try to understand what the problem could be. This can be done in many ways. You have to troubleshoot by attempting variation, for example:

Do not be perturbed if members of the audience are keeping themselves busy with writing or drawing: it could be nothing more than a concentration aid.

- Variation in voice: speak louder or faster.
- Variation in the use of visual aids: move on to another aid or turn aids on or off.
- Variation in the style of presenting: you could pause and ask a question to re-engage the audience's attention.
- Interrupt your presentation with an anecdote.
- Find reasons for the lack of interest. Grab hold of the audience by asking them to discuss an issue with the person next to them for a few seconds. Any form of action or interaction will do.
- If the audience is uncomfortable because the venue is too hot, ask for a window to be opened; if it is late in the day and the audience has participated in intensive sessions, ask your audience to stand up and stretch.

Distractions

Disasters will happen: flip charts falling over; you smashing the water jug from the table; a person in the audience collapses . . . .

Ignore it. Why should someone else's misfortune interrupt your presentation?

Acknowledge it. It happened. Then do something about it.

Don't ignore a distraction. See it as an opportunity in disguise. Acknowledge an accident by picking up the flip chart or jug. In the event of a person collapsing, ask for assistance. By showing care, you build credibility and your audience can see a human side that can only make them connect better with you. Once the people in the audience have calmed down, recap your last thought and carry on.

Comparing yourself to other presenters

Everybody else told a joke, so you start your presentation with the joke you heard on the radio drivetime show on your way to work. After telling it, you laugh the loudest.

Why do this to yourself in the first instance? Don't change your well-prepared presentation.

Don't try to tell a joke because everybody else told jokes. You will make yourself uncomfortable and erode your credibility. You need to be true to yourself and your personality. At this stage you are your own worst critic because of stress levels. For once don't take yourself too seriously. Each presentation is appreciated for what it is worth. After all your preparations, your presentation deserves to be heard. (If you did not prepare adequately, then you deserve to suffer through it.)

The content of your presentation is criticised

Criticise the person who attacked you with the same aggressiveness. If he can dish that, he should be able to take it back.

At least they acknowledge your presentation and will remember it. Some of the most severely criticised presentations we have heard ended up being the stepping stone for creative problem-solving options. Do you remember F W de Klerk's announcement of the release of Nelson Mandela? This announcement that changed our history was subjected to severe criticism from almost all sides. Listen to the feedback. Take from it what is constructive and learn from the criticism.

Look on the bright side: the audience listened. You provoked them.

Somebody launches a personal attack on you

Attack back as you know that in a situation like this attack is the best defence.

Personal attacks are a manifestation of bad taste in the person who launched the attack. Don't show worse taste by counter-attacking.

Be analytical: cut the attack short politely and manage the situation by focussing on factual issues you have raised in the presentation. Avoid further eye contact with the attacker.

Always remain polite and positive towards your audience.

QUESTIONS

Depending on the size of your audience, it may be appropriate to field questions during the body of the presentation. In some cases you will need to deal with questions then and there. In other cases you may indicate to the audience that you will be addressing that point later. You are the best person to judge how to handle this issue. Remember one thing: if you said you would address an issue later, then do it, otherwise you will have a serious credibility problem. Nothing will damage your credibility in the long run more than not keeping your word.

Nobody asks questions

There you are waiting in anticipation and nobody asks a question. This silence can be deafening and very awkward. Give the audience time to formulate their questions. You can pre-empt such a situation by leaving certain things unsaid in the presentation, which might lead to questions. Otherwise you can request a person beforehand to ask the first question. If you forewarn the audience that there will be a question-and-answer session, it will probably encourage people to formulate questions as the presentation proceeds. Another strategy is to ask the audience the first question and provoke them into discussion.

Ten questions are asked simultaneously

Write the questions down and take time to see how you can combine answers. In your answer, reiterate your main points.

You are asked a question that you cannot answer

Be honest. Say that you do not have an answer. Ask if anybody in the audience knows the answer. Only promise to find out and report back if the situation presents itself.

You need a few seconds to think about your answer

If, when put on the spot to answer a question or point, you come up blank then delaying tactics can buy you some time. But do not use these; only the true pawpaw of q&a would do the following:

- *'I think the answer to your last question will clear up your confusion on this subject. (Long pause) Are you ready?'*
- *'Excellent question, and I think the answer will startle you.' (Pause, look thoughtful as if a response is due.)*
- *'I'm glad you asked that. Would you like a long or short answer?'*
- *'Why do you ask that?' / 'What makes you ask that?'*

You could also echo the question back or ask the other person a similar or more difficult question:
'What do you think the answer to your question is?'

Another tactic is, with a sparkle in your eye, to launch into a long-winded story:
'This reminds me of the time I was in the middle of nowhere. Let me tell you, it was hot! (Time to think up real answer during dramatic pauses.) And we were in a small hotel when a gas leak started.
Well! You can imagine how we . . . .'

These tactics will seriously undermine your presentation and irritate your audience. Instead, be honest.

If you need time to think of an answer, tell your audience.

PITFALLS: HOW NOT TO ALIENATE YOUR AUDIENCE

You've worked hard on your presentation in order to inform your audience, convince them of your view, to get them to do what you want them to do. You've studied body language to know what they are feeling and how to use your body language to get the audience to relax and to pay attention to your presentation. However, in the heat of the moment, and in your state of nervousness, you may alienate your audience without realising it.

Never attack members of the audience verbally. Do not question their intelligence, their taste, their maturity (or lack of it), or make any personal comments.

- Never twist comments and questions around in your favour. 'Your last sentence ended with a preposition, please restate it properly,' is not the most acceptable way of answering somebody who may have disputed one of the points that you raised during your presentation. Respond to the question, not to your feelings about the question (or the person who asked it).
- Do not cast any doubts on the other person's competence.
- Do not use your knowledge of the other person's (private) life to get out of a sticky situation. 'What was it your ex-wife used to say?' – this most certainly has no bearing on the content of your presentation.
- If you can see where the other person's logic is leading, you can make it very difficult for them by arguing each minute subpoint and example. If the other person cannot get past the first point,

how will a case ever be made? But, before you take this approach, ask yourself one question: how constructive is this? We certainly don't recommend doing this.

IT AIN'T OVER TILL IT'S OVER

So, your presentation is over and done with. Keep in mind that you, however, are not done until the moment you are finally out of sight of the audience. A well-known doctor made a very impressive and emotional presentation about cancer. The hospital he worked for needed more money for cancer research. After his presentation, he stood outside the hall and smoked two cigarettes. Needless to say, that was too much for some of the sponsors. He never got the funding!

Remember, it's also important to provide your audience with a way to contact you. Be available, if possible, after your presentation for discussions or more questions, even if there was a question-and-answer session. Having a chat over a cup of tea afterwards gives you time for a one-on-one conversation – and the chance to wind down.

LAST WORDS

- Be alive and energetic.
- Be yourself.
- Be natural.
- Be appropriate at all times on all levels.
- Have a strong message with just as strong a delivery.

Six golden rules to remember when you present:

- Don't lie.
- Use credible and current evidence.

- Understand your own message.
- Be concrete.
- Be sure of your facts.
- Have fun!

All that is left for you now is to go out there and deliver the presentation of a lifetime.

Good luck and enjoy it!

RESOURCE LIST

BOOKS

Adler, H. 1996. *NLP for Managers.* Piatkus: London.

Allan & Bacon. 1997. *Delivery Dynamics.* A & B Public Speech.

Bradbury, Andrew. 1995. *Successful Presentation Skills.* Kogan Page: London.

Christopher, Elizabeth M. 1996. *Negotiating Skills for Business.* Kogan Page: London.

Davies, Philippa. 1990. *Your Total Image. How to communicate success.* Piatkus : London.

Denny, R. 1995. *Speak for Yourself.* Kogan Page: London.

Miller, Anne. 1998. *Presentation Jazz – How to make your sales presentation sing.* Amacom: New York.

Simpkins, Clive. 1995. *The Penguin Concise Communicator.* Penguin Books: London.

Stuart, Christina. 1988. *Effective Speaking. The essential guide to making the most of your communication skills.* Pan Books: London.

Walch, Sam. 1997. *II Steps of Effective Communication.* The Pennsylvania State University: Department of Speech Communication: Internet.

ECG, 1998: *Clean the Wax from your Words.* ECG Newsletter

ORGANISATIONS

Across Borders Arts Education: drama and voice training
Yolisa Dalamba
Tel: (011) 716 3706

The Communicator: voice and speech training programmes
Niki Seberini and Laura Moavero
Tel: (011) 887 5118

The Grooming School: finishing and communication training
Chante Hinds and Tselane Tambo
Tel: (011) 784 6081

Ronel Toerien Productions: voice and presentation training
Tel: (011) 888 7638

Toastmasters: Standard Bank Operations
1st Floor, Standard Bank Centre, 5 Simmonds Street
Tel: (011) 636 1069

Yooneek: multimedia design
Lauren Senior
Tel: 082 565 3255